CW00384621

Become a decision-maki
change your life forever, using…

The
Double Best
Method

You will never make a bad
choice again

Sophie Hannah

TABLE OF CONTENTS

AUTHOR'S NOTE

I want to draw your attention to something you might hardly have noticed — the four massive claims made on the cover and title page of this book:

1. that if you use The Double Best Method, you will become not merely good at making decisions, but a genius in the field;
2. that your life will be transformed by using this tool;
3. that you will never make a bad choice again;
4. that as soon you start practising this method, regret thoughts, and the pain they cause, will vanish from your life.

I bet some of you skipped past all of that, thinking, 'Yeah, yeah. All self-help books swear to be life-changing and they rarely are.'

I agree. I've never understood why writers and publishers market books using claims about them that aren't true.

This book will keep all of the grand promises made in its marketing taglines. All you need to do is start using The Double Best Method, and your life will change in the most brilliant way. Try it and see.

For anyone wondering if I wrote this book because decision-making is one of my superpowers…nope. My reasons were the exact opposite of that. This is a self-help book in the truest sense — I was the person who desperately needed this particular help.

For a large part of my life so far, I have been terrible at deciding. The freer I am to choose, the harder I find it. This doesn't mean I have made mainly bad choices in my life — that's definitely not the case. But for most of my 51 years, I have resisted making decisions for as long as possible. I've made brilliant choices with great enthusiasm while simultaneously believing my reasons were probably unhinged. And I've done the opposite plenty of times too: made awful choices that I was convinced must be absolutely correct, even though I felt doubtful and full of dread. I never trusted myself to know if I was doing the right thing. Before The Double Best Method, I wouldn't have dreamed of allowing myself wholeheartedly to approve of any choice I made. I used to torment myself endlessly with the question 'What if I'm a big fool who's just wrecked everything?'

That's why I needed a Firm Policy (with capital letters for added firmness) that works brilliantly 100% of the time. That's what The Double Best Method is. My judgement in any individual situation no longer needs to be wise or correct, because the policy is infallible. If you use it, and follow the steps as outlined, *you cannot get it wrong*.

By now you must be wondering: what on earth is this magic process? For those of you who are short of time and want to get the formula straight away, I understand, and I'm not going to make you wait any longer for the answer. Skip the Introduction and head directly for Chapter 1, which contains the Double Best decision-making method in full. One of the amazing things about this tool is that it will work brilliantly for you whether you understand why it works or not. In this way *and in this way only* it resembles the general anaesthetic I was given when I had dental surgery as a child. That blighter knocked me out before I could count to ten, even though I had no idea what was injected into me or why it had the effect on me that it did.

Using The Double Best Method takes no effort or practice. It's as easy as making a cup of tea: you simply have to know the steps and then do them in the right order. You can use this formula to make any decision, big or small, for the rest of your life. That's what I do. Since I invented the method almost by accident, I have Double-Bested nearly every choice I've made.

For those of you who are not short of time, I strongly recommend that you read all of this book, because knowing the hows and whys of The Double Best Method will make you so thrilled to use it, you'll find yourself actively hoping that life throws ever more challenging decision-making predicaments at you. Yes, really. You will have boundless confidence in your ability to make the trickiest choices using this formula, and to get them right every time, and you will feel positively gleeful knowing that you'll never again have that horrible feeling of being stuck in indecision and seeing no way out.

So, does everyone know where they're headed next? If you want the simple step-by-step formula, Chapter 1 is the place to go. If you're curious about how a best-selling mystery fiction writer in Cambridge,

England, ended up inventing a unique and life-changing decision-making tool almost by accident, read on…

INTRODUCTION

Significant Millions

I made my first Double-Best decision in July 2012, many years before I officially invented the method. I had no clue, at the time, that I was making a Double Best choice.

Here's the short version of what happened: I was offered a 99% chance of losing £35,000, which was also a 1% chance of making significant millions. It was made very clear to me that, if I said yes, those were my odds. If I said no, there was a 100% chance that I would *not* lose my £35,000; I would get to keep it and spend it on all the things in life that cost money: groceries, paying bills, holidays, my mortgage.

I was offered this chance by someone who wanted and needed an answer quickly. As was my custom at the time, I put off making the decision for as long as I could, which was not very long. I remember thinking, 'I wish I had more time to decide.' But I didn't. This person that I liked and respected a lot needed an answer, and I didn't want to keep him waiting.

I chose the 99% chance of losing and the 1% chance of winning that came with it. If I had not made that particular choice for what I thought of then as 'my own strange reasons' — reasons that I told myself at the time were too absurd and naïve to share with anyone apart from my husband — I would never have thought more deeply about the underlying principles that had influenced my decision.

I got lucky. In July 2021, after a wait of 9 years, the best-case-scenario result happened and I made an amount of money that made me want to pinch myself every day for at least six months, to check I wasn't dreaming.

Here's the really interesting part: I knew from the moment I decided to hand over the £35,000 *that I could not lose.* Oh, I could lose all the money I'd invested, for sure; I knew that I very likely would. But nevertheless, there existed within me a deep groove of conviction that

I could not lose as long as I continued to think about the choice I'd made in the 'bonkers' way that had informed my choice to take the risk. I said to my husband, 'I know this is a highly eccentric way to think about it, so please don't tell anyone why I'm doing this' — that's how convinced I was that my reasoning was probably ridiculous.

When do you think I stopped referring to my decision to part with the £35,000 as 'bonkers', while laughing at myself in a self-deprecating way? I'm guessing most of you will say, 'July 2021, obviously — when the super-unlikely win result landed.'

Actually, it was in 2018, when I heard one of the world's most successful life and business coaches talking about the value of money. Her name is Brooke Castillo, and I had been introduced to her podcast, *The Life Coach School,* by a friend. I was working my way through it, episode by episode, and had become a passionate fan. The episodes had titles like 'Why You Aren't Taking Action', 'How To Feel Better' and 'Success vs. Happiness'. I did not listen to them in chronological order, because there's something about chronological anything that makes me feel stifled and restricted

(Weird, right? I blame myself and not chronology for this.)

I had listened to approximately a hundred and fifty episodes of Brooke's podcast and was already familiar with her approach to life, and her way of thinking, by the time I got round to Episode 24, *Money Problems*.

Here's what I heard Brooke say in that episode:

'Money is absolutely neutral. I know that that's hard for some of you to believe, but money is just paper that just lays there. It's just a digital readout on your screen…That piece of paper, in and of itself, has no value until we assign it value and agree on that value.

That's really important to recognize, because everything else is just our thinking about it. I'm often reminded of the whole Bernie Madoff scandal and thinking about all of these people who went all of these years believing that they had millions of dollars…They would look at the falsified reports. They would look at their screens, and they would see that they had all this money, and they were feeling very abundant, and they were feeling very secure.

Now, they didn't really have the money, right? This whole time they were being lied to. That money had been long spent, so it wasn't having the money that was giving them this feeling of security, right? Because they didn't actually have it. The only thing giving them the feeling of security and abundance was their belief that they had it.

Why is this important to look at? Because it's really important to separate that it's not your money that you have in your bank account that makes you feel a certain way. It is your thinking about your money in your bank account that makes you feel a certain way.

People will say, "If I had a million dollars, I would feel secure." I say to them, "The million dollars doesn't make you feel secure. The million dollars just sits there. Your thought about what it means to have a million dollars is what makes you feel secure."'

As I listened, it struck me that all these ideas were highly relevant to my £35,000 decision of 2012. Putting them together with other things I had heard Brooke say in different episodes of her podcast, I had a startling realisation: *Brooke Castillo would not have thought my £35,000 gamble was ridiculous. She would have thought I made a brilliant decision.* (I have never sought confirmation of this from the woman herself, but I know I'm right.)

I was stunned by this revelation. Sitting alone in the lounge of my house in Cambridge, England, I actually gasped when it struck me. Triumphantly, I announced to an empty room, 'Maybe I'm not as ridiculous as I think I am!' And then I thought to myself (because there's a limit to how much even I am willing to say out loud to an audience of sofas, chairs and an occasional table), 'Maybe risking that £35,000 was not reckless but actually the wise and smart thing to do, *even if I lose it all.* Brooke Castillo would think so, if I explained to her why I did it.' (Remember, this was 2018 — three years before that gamble turned into wildest-dreams profit in 2021; after that happened, everyone on the planet would have thought I'd made the right choice.)

I went back and listened again to that same section of Episode 24 of Brooke's podcast, about Bernie Madoff and the difference between money and our beliefs about money. Meticulously, I tried to recreate my exact thought process from 2012, the one that had led me to make the decision I made.

Yes, I was right. Yes, Brooke Castillo would definitely have approved.

And then two strange words appeared in my mind, words I hadn't thought about for decades. They surfaced from the murkiest depths of my memory: two words that were connected to a famous man who was born in 1921 and went on to die in 2002, ten years before I took my £35,000 gamble.

I was pretty sure these two words were not in any dictionary. I remembered a conversation I'd had with my dad about them, on a family holiday in 1984. I was thirteen at the time, and my dad and I were at the beach — in the sea, in fact. I wasn't at all aware of having this memory still stored in my mind until I listened to Episode 24 of Brooke Castillo's podcast and started to think about it in connection with my choice to take a £35,000 risk.

When I put all these things together in 2018, a tentative theory started to take shape in my mind, about the difference between legendary and lamentable decision-making. Five years of mulling and experimentation followed, and finally The Double Best Method was born.

If you are keen to hear all the stories I've alluded to (what were my 'bonkers' reasons for risking £35k when I was 99% certain to lose it all? On what did I spend that money? What were the two strange words? Who is the famous dead man?), don't worry. I'm going to share all of these essential anecdotes with you later. First, though, I'm going to tell you about The Double Best Method — partly, as I've said, for those you with time constraints who want to get the essentials immediately, but also because the main point of this book is to introduce you to this very easy decision-making formula, so that you can start using it straight away.

Then later, as you learn more about the powerful philosophy behind The Double Best Method, you'll be able to test whether that makes a difference or not. Does Double Best decision-making become even more rewarding and effective once you know the reasoning behind it? I can't wait to hear what you think.

Now, though, let's get to the specifics of the Method…

Chapter 1

The Double Best Method — How To Do It

Here, in five simple steps, is the Double Best decision-making formula:

Step 1: Write down all the options you're choosing between.

It might be only two, or it might be eight. This method works for choices involving any and all numbers of options.

Step 2: For each one, write down the Best Possible Outcome that choosing that option might give you.

There's no need to think about probabilities, or likelihood of outcomes. We will discuss how these two important issues relate to Double Best Decision-Making later. For now, we're thinking only about possibility. For example, the Best Possible Outcome of proposing marriage to Prince William, heir to the throne of Great Britain (assuming you were irretrievably in love with him and wanted, more than you want anything else in the world, to be his spouse), is that he would say yes, divorce Catherine, the Princess of Wales, and marry you instead at his earliest convenience.

Another important note: 'best' in the context of The Double Best Method *always and only* means 'your favourite/your preferred'. No one else needs to agree with you that the Best Possible Outcome would be for you to end up married to Prince William. Nor do you need to believe you are correct to have it as your favourite outcome. It simply needs to be your strong preference in order to be considered 'best' for our purposes.

Step 3: Choose your favourite of the Best Possible Outcomes, however many there are.

This is where the name 'Double Best' comes from: you're choosing the **Best** Possible Outcome that you like **best**.

So, your list of Best Possible Outcomes (BPOs) might look like this:

Option 1 — Ask Prince William to marry me

- - - Best Possible Outcome: I live happily ever after with Prince William.

Option 2 — Don't ask Prince William to marry me, and instead say yes to the marriage proposal from Dylan from my work.

- - - Best Possible Outcome: I live happily ever after with Dylan from my work.

Option 3 — Don't ask Prince William to marry me, and say no to the marriage proposal from Dylan at work.

- - - Best Possible Outcome: If and when I want to, I marry someone else and live happily ever after with that person. Or I remain happily single by choice forever.

In this example, you'd be choosing between three BPOs, but somebody else with a similar decision to make might have five options on their list; they might also be quite tempted to propose marriage to Lady Gaga and Cristiano Ronaldo.

However many Best Possible Outcomes you've written down, Step 3 is that you choose your favourite: your Double Best, the best of all the bests. It doesn't matter why it's your favourite, or which you think you *should* prefer, and would, if only you were a better person; it's the one that you — actual you, as you are now — desire most and are most attracted to, no matter the reason.

Step 4: Once you've chosen your Double Best option — the one that gives you the possibility of your favourite of all the BPOs, ask yourself:' What is the Worst Possible Outcome (WPO) of my choosing this option?' and write down your answer.

In the case of proposing marriage to Prince William, your answer might be:

a)   being rejected or ignored by Prince William

or it could be:

b)   attracting the loathing of millions of people all over the world for being the brazen creature who deliberately set out to destroy the marriage of the Prince and Princess of Wales.

Step 5: Ask yourself: is the risk of this WPO worth taking, in order to stand a chance of getting my Double Best outcome?

If your answer is 'Yes, definitely,' then your choice is made.

If your answer is 'No', then eliminate that option and select the one from your list that offers a chance of your next favourite BPO. Repeat this process until your answer to the question in Step 5 is 'Yes, definitely'. Your decision is made as soon as you've chosen a Double Best option that has a WPO you're willing or even happy to risk creating. (Later, we will look at what to do when every option has, or seems to have, an intolerable WPO attached to it.)

§§§

That's how to do it, and it's all the information you need in order to get started as a Double Best decision maker. (And if you want, immediately, to understand why this method is as brilliant and foolproof as it is, please make your way immediately to Chapter 10, where this is explained in full.)

For the keen puzzle-solvers among you, I have a question: now that you know the method: can you figure out, even before having practised it at all, why this approach to decision-making works so well? There are ten main reasons I've managed to identify, and maybe there are some more that I haven't yet thought of. If you'd like to take a guess at what some of those reasons might be, I'd love to hear from you — put down this book and email me right now at sophie@sophiehannah.com. Just don't forget to pick up the book and carry on reading afterwards!

And finally, for those of you who would rather not strain your brains trying to guess anything, don't worry. I get it — you're the audience. You want to stay in your seats, eating popcorn, not climb on stage. That's fine. All will soon be revealed. In the coming chapters, we're going to look at the many reasons why The Double Best Method works so well and test precisely how it works with many different examples.

First, though, let's deal with two issues that appear to be (but, luckily, are not) potential flaws in the formula…

Chapter 2

The Flaws That Aren't Flaws

Before I started to write this book, I spent months stress-testing The Double Best Method. Early in this process, I tried it out on a friend and ran smack-bang into two potential stumbling blocks that I should probably have seen coming a mile off but, weirdly, did not.

My friend had been offered a new job (let's call it Job A) with a salary that was 30k a year more than he was earning in his present job. At the same time, he had also just applied for another new job, Job B, which had the same salary as Job A and which he thought he would marginally prefer. However, he wouldn't know if he had got Job B for another six weeks.

He couldn't decide how to respond to the offer of Job A. Should he tell that company that he wouldn't be able to give them an answer for six weeks because he had another job application in the pipeline? Or should he say yes to Job A, tell them nothing about Job B, and then hand in his notice at Job A, a mere six weeks after accepting it, if it turned out that the Job B company also wanted him?

Excitedly, I told him about The Double Best Method, and, in a Zoom chat, we laid out his options and their BPOs:

Option 1 — Take Job A, and say nothing about maybe giving notice in six weeks time in order to move to Job B.

- - - Best Possible Outcome: Job A is secured, and there's no risk of the company saying, 'No, sorry, we don't want to wait six weeks for your decision. Goodbye.' And if he is then offered Job B, there's nothing stopping him taking it. Either way, there's no risk of him ending up without a new job that is 30k a year more lucrative than his current job.

Option 2 — Say, 'I'm very interested, but I'm afraid I'm not going to be able to let you know for six weeks.'

- - - Best Possible Outcome: the Job A people say, 'That's absolutely fine. We will happily wait six weeks and keep our offer open until then.' So Job A is secured, he still has the option of taking Job B instead if it's offered, and he doesn't have to worry about misleading anyone by withholding relevant information, or risk having to disappoint the Job A company by perhaps handing in his notice only a few weeks after being appointed.

'What if I don't know which is my favourite of the Best Possible Outcomes?' my friend asked.

'Oh,' I replied, crestfallen. 'I think you might just have broken my brand new decision-making method.'

Thankfully he had not...

What if you can't choose between the BPOs of the available options?

The solution to this is incredibly simple. If you don't have a Favourite BPO, that mean both options win. Think of a race in which two runners cross the finish line at exactly the same moment. Do we award those runners joint second prize? No, of course not. They are both first prize winners.

If the options you're choosing between all jointly win first prize, and you truly have not even a smidgeon of preference for any of them, then toss a coin to decide the matter.

If you do so and find that a small voice deep inside you whispers, 'Oh, no' when it hears the verdict, then it turns out you *did* have a preference after all — one you were unaware of until a coin toss chose an option you like less, as it turns out. Great! So now you know which you prefer.

$$$

Further discussion soon revealed that my friend did indeed know what his preferred BPO was: he wanted to secure Job A now, no matter what happened with Job B. He did not want to risk the offer of Job A being withdrawn.

'Great,' I said. 'So now we move on to the next question: what is the WPO (Worst Possible Outcome) of choosing the option that secures Job A for you immediately?'

'The worst outcome is that I then get offered Job B as well,' he said. 'And I take Job B, and everyone at the Job A company finds out that I knew I was in the running for Job B when I accepted Job A, and kept it secret. Word starts to spread that I'm sneaky and manipulative, and I lose my good reputation.'

'Okay,' I said, 'And so on to the next stage of The Double Best Method: is the risk of that WPO worth taking, in order to get the Double Best outcome of knowing Job A is in the bag?'

At this point my friend tried once more to break The Double Best Method. 'I don't know,' he said. 'What does the method say you should do if you don't know if it's worth the risk?'

'Help!' I thought to myself. 'This is a problem. The people who need The Double Best Method most are those who struggle to make decisions — so of course they will have difficulty 'and deciding which BPO they prefer, and whether the WPO associated with that option is worth the risk.'

At the time, I didn't know how to answer my friend's question, so I told him I'd go away and think about it, and off I went to do some detailed mulling.

I came back to him a few days later and said, 'Let's look at the WPO offered by the other option: what would that be?'

'The Job A people say, "Sorry, we can't wait six weeks for your decision," and then I'd either have to say yes on the spot to Job A, and take myself out of the running for Job B, or I'd need to accept that I'd lost Job A and also might not get Job B. I might end up with no new job.'

'So the worst case scenario there is the status quo?' I said. 'You stay in your current job?'

'Yes,' he said. 'And the worst case scenario of the other option is I end up in a job that pays 30k more a year, but my reputation might be trashed because I'd have been shady and not upfront in my dealings with people. Hmm,' he said. 'Actually, that would be much worse than the status quo. Because I like the job I'm in now, and the money's not bad, and I like it that other people think well of me. Most of all, I like that I think well of myself. I wouldn't be able to do that any more if I knew I'd been slightly dishonest with the Job A people by saying, "Yes, please," to their job offer while saying nothing about Job B.'

His choice was made. Even though he hadn't at first been able to choose between the two BPOs, he *could* choose between the WPOs; one was an intolerable prospect for him, so he chose the option that didn't have it as a possible outcome.

In the end, he was offered Job A, accepted it, and withdrew immediately from the Job B application process.

Notice how the option he chose was neither of the two listed above. He picked a third option:

Option 3 — Say yes immediately to Job A and rule out Job B altogether.

Before making a Double Best Decision, make sure to think hard about what all the options are. There might be one that you've not thought of. When you think you've listed them all, ask yourself, 'Is that it? Is there anything else I could do here? What other choices are open to me?

§§§

So, that's what you do if you don't know whether the WPO of your Double Best choice is worth risking in order to stand a chance of getting your Double Best outcome. Is the WPO attached to your next favourite BPO something you're much more willing to risk? If so, are you willing to forego the chance of getting your favourite of the BPOs, and settle for the option that gives you a slightly less desired BPO — maybe your second favourite — but definitely avoids your least favourite WPO?

If your answer to that question is yes, then your decision is made.

If your answer is no, then you've reached the point where you need to look at all the BPO and WPO outcomes attached to each option as pairs, and choose your favourite pair.

§§§

Choosing a favourite downside might seem like an odd idea, but it is what we do each time we make a decision. We cannot know the future or predict with infallible accuracy what our choice might lead to in terms of outcomes, so the only wise way to make decisions is to consider carefully the potential-upside-plus-potential-downside combinations we're choosing between.

It's pointless to say, 'I am unwilling to risk any downside at all, of any sort,' because no choice we make is ever going to create 100% perfection in our lives. Even winning twenty million pounds in the National Lottery would have downsides attached to it (worrying about which stocks and shares to invest in; how can you give a million to your brother Tommy, whom you love, without also giving the same amount to your brother Jimmy, whom you loathe? Imagine the extended family ructions if you gave a million to Tommy and not to Jimmy! It doesn't bear thinking about, frankly.)

Sometimes, either directly or indirectly, we refuse to choose. If you're interested in reading a superb and very short novel in which the protagonist does exactly this, I heartily recommend Herman Melville's *Bartleby the Scrivener*, one of my favourite books of all time. If

Bartleby had used The Double Best Method, there's no doubt in my mind that he would have ended up in a better situation.

Refusing to choose, or simply numbing out and not noticing that you're failing to choose anything in an active way, is a choice. It's important that we realise that. Strictly speaking, we can and should list 'Doing absolutely nothing' as an additional option in our Double Best options assessments, and look at the BPO and WPO of Not Choosing.

If your Double Best analysis of the available choices leads you to the conclusion that none of the WPOs are worth risking, then it's highly likely that you're trying to reject reality. You are effectively declaring yourself unwilling to accept the reality that your actions might lead to things you might not like. That's a little like saying I don't want to breathe ever again in case one day I inhale a fly.

§§§

A note about the 'Worth The Risk' part of the equation

Deciding that the Worst Possible Outcome attached to your BPO option is worth the risk does not mean that the WPO would be insignificant, not that bad, or barely a problem at all. Sometimes we are going to want to say, 'Yes, it's worth risking this WPO,' even when we know the WPO would be absolutely horrendous if it were to happen. Decisions to stand up and protest against injustice often fall into this category: we might know that the WPO is that we'll get arrested, beaten, even killed, but we're unwilling to choose the option with the even worse WPO attached to it: we say nothing and act as cowardly bystander-colluders in the face of great evil.

The truth is, taking risks and occasionally coming up against downsides can be good for us. Don't we want to take the risk that we might grow our skills, our creativity and mental agility, our resilience, our strength of character, our virtuous moral qualities? Challenging situations, replete with downsides, are the very means by which we get to do that. Each time we decide we're willing to risk a significant WPO in order to stretch ourselves and aim for our favourite BPO, one of two things will happen: either we'll create amazing results that we love, or else we will have a chance to learn and grow as humans and become more resilient, which will stand us in very good stead and increase our chance of success next time we're ready to aim high.

That, of course, is assuming we want to aim high, or indeed aim at all. Not everyone does. Some people would far rather play it safe and have an easy life that do anything too risky or bold. And, as we'll see in the next chapter, what's a great choice for them might not be a great choice for us.

Chapter 3

Who Do You Want To Be?

One thing I would ask my friend today, if I were doing a Double Best analysis of his choices with him, is: 'Who do you want to be in this situation?'

I didn't ask him that question when we had the conversation, because I hadn't yet fully developed the Double Best Method, but he answered it anyway. It was his strong idea of who he wanted to be that enabled him to choose between the options. He wanted to be someone who cared more about his integrity than an extra 30k a year.

Who we want to be is one of the many things we get to choose when following the Double Best process. And, unlike the outcomes that might be created by our decisions, it's something we can always control. In any situation, however challenging, and no matter how much of it is beyond our control, we can always think to ourselves, 'Who do I want to be in this circumstance?' and then be that person.

Here's an illustration of this very principle in action: some years ago, I hired a private detective to find out some information that I believed I would be unable to find out for myself; there had been many lies, and I wanted the truth. When I told a close friend that I had done this, she said, 'Oh, my God. Don't tell anyone, ever, that you hired a detective.'

'Why not?' I said.

'Because you don't want people to think you're the kind of person who would hire a detective,' she said, as if it should have been obvious.

'But I *am* that kind of person, clearly,' I pointed out. 'Because I *did* hire a detective.'

'Yes, but you don't want other people to know that,' she said, sounding rather frantic and breathless.

'Why not?' I said.

It took me some years to work out why that conversation had not made complete sense to either of us. My friend places a far higher value than I do on being and seeming normal, behaving conventionally and fitting in. For years, one of her regular complaints about the crime novels I write has been that they are 'not everywoman-ish enough' (my female protagonists are often ruthless, bizarre, obsessive). If this friend of mine wrote novels, I have no doubt that their protagonists would be regular good sorts who never put a foot wrong or do anything eccentric-verging-on-bonkers.

She would absolutely hate to think that anyone might call her behaviour outrageous or raise eyebrows about anything she'd done. I, in contrast, love nothing more than when people say to me, 'Only you would think to do a thing like that! I don't know anyone else who would dare do X, Y or Z.'

I even wrote a poem celebrating my own outrageous streak that has attracted much love from hundreds (maybe even thousands, by now) of my fellow outrageous and aspiring-outrageous types over the years:

IF PEOPLE DISAPPROVE OF YOU...

Make being disapproved of your hobby.
Make being disapproved of your aim.
Devise new ways of scoring points
in the Being Disapproved Of Game.

Let them disapprove in their dozens.
Let them disapprove in their hordes.
You'll find that being disapproved of
builds character, brings rewards,

just like any form of striving.
Don't be arrogant; don't coast
on your high disapproval rating.
Try to be disapproved of most.

At this point, if it's useful,
draw a pie chart or a graph.
Show it to someone who disapproves.
When they disapprove, just laugh.

Count the emotions you provoke:
anger, suspicion, shock.
One point for each of these and two
for every boat you rock.

Feel yourself warming to your task –
you do it bloody well.
At last you've found an area
in which you can excel.

Savour the thrill of risk without
the fear of getting caught.
Whether they sulk or scream or pout,
enjoy your new-found sport.

Meanwhile all those who disapprove
while you are having fun
won't even know your game exists
so tell yourself you've won.

Outrageousness and outlandishness, as it turns out, are two of my core values (I'm only slightly joking, folks), especially when they're in the service of solving problems that otherwise might remain unsolved. I have countless stories to prove it — like this one, which I still smile about years later and included in my novel *Haven't They Grown*, attached to a character who was well-known for his outrageousness:

In 2001, my husband and I spent a fortnight on the Greek island of Skyros, where I was teaching a creative writing course. There was no swimming pool where we were staying, and going to the beach involved what I regarded as sweaty hiking rather than the kind of easy walking that I prefer.

Much nearer, there was a hotel, the Nefeli, that had a swimming pool that was always empty when we walked past it. I went in one day and asked if we could use it. 'No,' said the receptionist. Only the hotel's guests were allowed to use the pool. I offered to pay a daily fee, pointing out that the hotel appeared to have no guests, or at least not ones who liked swimming. I had never seen a single person in that pool. It was empty — a huge, gleaming aquamarine, shimmering in the sunlight — as the receptionist and I had this conversation.

She kept saying no, and I kept offering her more and more money, but to no avail. My husband, who was with me, muttered in my ear, 'Leave it, Soph. There's nothing we can do.'

If anything is likely to inspire me to greater outrageousness, it is the words 'There's nothing we can do.'

I asked the receptionist if there was a room available at the hotel for the next ten days. She looked confused. 'You want to stay here?' she said.

'No, I'm not going to be staying here,' I explained. 'I have to stay in the centre where I'm teaching. But I want to book a room for ten days, because it's the only way I can use the pool.'

I booked the room. It cost the equivalent of around £600. In 2001, that was a lot of money for me and my husband to spend. But I was willing to go without other things once I got back to England — takeaways, new clothes, haircuts, whatever — if it meant I could swim in this gorgeous hotel pool every day for the rest of my time on Skyros.

We only ever used the hotel for around ten minutes a day, to change into our swimming costumes and then out of them again. Many people who have heard this story think it was a ridiculous waste of money, but they are wrong. It was possibly the best £600 I have ever spent.

Why? Because of my core values…

Core Values

I didn't think much about Core Values until I did a Core Values Masterclass with American life coach Tiffany Han. She gave us a list to choose from and it took me a while, but I finally managed to make my various lists: top three, top ten. (Hierarchies matter in Core Values Land.)

I was excited to discover that my number one Core Value was Abundance. This knowledge made sense of so much in my life:

Why did I hire a private detective? Because I knew that an abundance of truth and knowledge was available, and that I was being deprived of it by lies.

Why did I pay £600 for a hotel room I didn't need in order to use a beautiful swimming pool? Because there was an abundance of swimming perfection that I would otherwise have missed out on. And even though I was far from well off at that time in my life, I felt as if more money was bound to turn up soon, from somewhere. I had always had that belief, even as a student with a large overdraft. My sister used to argue with me about it: 'More money *does not* always just turn up,' she said. 'You're massively in debt! Stop going to restaurants every night!' I lived in Rusholme, Manchester, at the time and was determined to benefit from the abundance of delicious curry that was to be found only minutes from my house.

It might not surprise you to hear that numbers 2 and 3 of my Top Three Core Values, after Abundance, are Freedom and Creativity. Do the above behaviours not sound exactly like what someone who wanted to be free (of conventional expectations and restrictions) and creative (finding ingenious ways to get the desired result) might do?

In the next chapter, I'm going to tell you all about the 35k gamble I took in 2012, and you will hopefully notice how these same three values played a part there too.

§§§

So, to summarise what precisely these last two chapters contribute to the Double Best formula: if we can't decide *either* which is our favourite of the available BPOs, *or* if the risk of a WPO is worth taking or not, there are two more essential steps that we can add to the decision-making process in order to clarify this:

Step 6: Ask yourself, 'Which option takes me closer to being who I want to be?'

Step 7: Identify your Core Values and then work out which option is most in line with them. Long lists of core values to choose from can be found in abundance by searching online.

Chapter 4

The RoboDoc Gamble

O kay, so…this seems like the right moment to tell you the full story of my £35,000 gamble, because that unlikely (though entirely factual) tale is the perfect example of Double Best thinking in action — even though I didn't realise it until many years later.

In February 2010, my family and I moved from West Yorkshire to Cambridge, and someone told us that St Catherine's College, Cambridge, had a girls choir

Our daughter, Phoebe, wanted to audition for this choir. She had (has) a beautiful singing voice but had never had any formal musical training, so we decided to find her a singing teacher. I searched online, found a woman who seemed impressive — Jessica, an American Mezzo-Soprano — and booked a first lesson. This led to many more, and during each one, while I waited to drive

Phoebe home, I sat in Jessica's lounge and chatted to her husband, Luke.

Luke was a scientist and worked for a company that made technological products. He told me that one of his current projects was creating a shower that was also a kind of disco, complete with music and lights.

'Huh!' I said, surprised. 'And...do you think you'll be able to do it?' I didn't understand why the client couldn't shower first, then go to a disco later, but I was well aware that an attitude like that would never lead to great innovation.

'Definitely,' Luke said with confidence.

'Wow.' I immediately labelled him in my mind as 'a clever, science-y type.' Then I made a suggestion, based on what I knew clever, science-y types sometimes did. 'Why don't you start your own company and invent an amazing new thingy — a product of some kind. Then, a few years later, you could sell that company for squillions of dollars.'

I had two friends who had done precisely this. One was a brilliant scientist like Luke, and the other was a brilliant IT/software person. They had sold their start-ups to GlaxoSmithKline and Intel respectively and made…well, I didn't know exactly how much, but I knew it was a squillions-ish amount in both cases.

I don't think I'd have made my suggestion to Luke if I hadn't been powerfully aware that creating world-changing technology was a) super cool and b) something I would never be able to it do myself. If you've read Charles Dickens's *Great Expectations*, you might recall that Miss Havisham urged young, beautiful Estella to break men's hearts. She knew she would need a proxy in order to achieve her goal, being far too old and cobwebby herself. I was neither old nor cobwebby, but I was crap at science: a confirmed arty type who would probably never be able to remember whether the degrees in physics were called Kevin or Kelvin.

As a writer of poetry and crime fiction, I knew that GlaxoSmithKline would be unlikely ever to want to buy a set of my detective novels for squillions, even if I offered them signed first editions and threw in free tickets to my next event at the Cheltenham Literature Festival.

Luke, however, was not restricted in the way that I was, and so it seemed to me that inventing an amazing, world-changing something-or-other should definitely be on his to-do list.

'Oh, no,' he said modestly. 'I doubt I could think of anything that ground-breaking. Anyway, I'm fine where I am.'

'Don't be silly. Of course you could do it,' I insisted. 'You just need to come up with a brilliant idea.'

'Hmm.' He looked sceptical.

More than a year later, I was in a Boston hotel room (I was on tour promoting my newest book in America) and got a call from a number I didn't recognise. It was Luke. He sounded very excited, and told me he'd had an idea for an incredible new invention that, if all went well, would revolutionise the surgical robotics industry. He wanted to leave his job and start his own company, exactly as I'd suggested to him all those months ago.

'Great!' I said. 'You should totally do it.'

'Yes, but there's a snag,' he said. 'As things stand, I can't afford to give up my job. If I'm going to do this and stand a chance of making it work, I need to be able to devote myself to it full-time. I need seed capital. And, er, you're the only person I know who has any money at all. And since me doing this was your idea in the first place, I thought…well, I thought you might want to be the company's first financial backer. You'd get lots of shares if you did, obviously.'

What he was asking for was £35,000. That would be enough to keep him going, he told me, while he took the initial first steps towards getting this new venture off the ground. He would then need to find a much bigger investor who could give him several million pounds, and he would need to find that person before my 35k of seed capital ran out, or else financial pressure would force him to get another job in order to keep a roof over his and his family's heads.

His brilliant idea was a small robot, of a similar shape to a human arm, that would perform laparoscopic surgery in a way that no existing surgical robot could. I immediately gave it the nickname 'RoboDoc', and I have called it that ever since.

I told Luke I'd think about it, hoping to be able to put off, for as long as possible, what sounded like a potentially expensive decision — because that was my habit in those days; my go-to first choice was almost always running away, hiding, and hoping the decision would somehow make itself without me having to do anything or take responsibility.

'Think quickly,' Luke said. 'This is time-sensitive. There's a strong chance that several tech companies are already working on new surgical robots, and if they get there first, we might have missed our chance forever.'

I didn't like the sound of that at all. Though I wouldn't have put it to myself in these terms at the time, Missing Amazing Chances Forever was very much not one of my Core Values.

I got back from America and discussed the RoboDoc possibility with my husband, who pointed out that I had already made an emotional investment in this yet-to-be-started company if I'd given it a nickname.

Luke came round and explained his plans and ideas in as much detail as two people with one science O-level between them could understand. He showed us some sketches he had drawn of RoboDoc. I think I probably said, 'Awww, he looks so cute!', because that is the kind of serious-minded tech investor I aspired to be, clearly.

Luke was very direct about the risk my husband and I would be taking if we said yes. Most start-ups fail, he told us, and there was no getting around that hard fact. It was overwhelmingly likely that, in spite of his best efforts, RoboDoc would fail and we would lose our money.

'What if it all goes really well?' I said. 'How big and amazing could this be?'

'Oh, huge,' said Luke. 'It could transform the field of medical robotics and make surgery vastly better, easier to perform. It could make a huge difference to medical outcomes for millions of people all over the world. The company could end up being worth billions.'

'*Billions*?' I said.

'Yes, but that's wildest dreams territory,' said Luke. 'As I say, there's a strong chance that won't happen and you'll lose...

'Yes, yes, we'll lose money,' I said, too excited by the best case scenario to worry all that much about the worst possible outcome. My gut instinct was telling me that this was a great thing to try and make work, whether or not we succeeded.

Luke also explained that our investment would probably be eligible for something called EIS, which would mean we'd get some of the money back in the form of tax relief.

We said yes, and became the first financial backers of Luke's new business. A few days later, I started to look on Zillow.com for houses called things like 'Red Rock Ranch' in the Arizona desert, with swimming pools that glowed like turquoise jewels, and views of cacti and pink canyons. Since the dream-come-true scenario for RoboDoc was statistically very unlikely to happen, I wanted to make the absolute most of this time I had now — the time during which I could believe that it was definitely going to happen because I knew how brilliant Luke was, and if anyone could make it work, he could.

I had no idea at the time, but this was the beginning of my Double Best thinking habit. Unless and until Luke told me, 'Sorry, but the whole enterprise has failed and it's all over,' my plan was to believe that the best case scenario was for sure the one we were heading for. Hence my Zillow searches. I told my husband I was looking for 'our RoboDoc house'. He probably thought I was indulging in an unrealistic fantasy but, as I saw it, I was simply *believing*: in Luke, in RoboDoc's potential and in the dream of huge success. I was unable to foresee the future, and I decided I might as well believe it would all go swimmingly, since there was no data to prove me wrong.

Hands up who's thinking: what about the discouraging statistics? That data, as far as I could see, told me nothing about what would be the fate of any individual start-up. Even if only one per cent of start-ups succeeded, there was no way of knowing whether RoboDoc would be in that 1% or in the 99% that failed. No statistical study had ever produced the result of 'Sophie's friend Luke is unlikely to succeed', nor examined the belief and determination levels of those involved, nor analysed which of them were or were not obsessive and deluded best-case-scenario dreamers who also happened to be incredibly stubborn and unwilling to admit defeat.

I allowed myself to be guided by what felt to me like two big clues — Luke's brilliant, inventive mind and his boundless energy and enthusiasm for making it work. If anyone was likely to get into the 1% success group, it was him. As I saw it, there was absolutely nothing concrete or factual preventing me from believing that RoboDoc could achieve wildest-dreams level success.

A few weeks later, I spoke to Luke and asked him if he too regularly looked on Zillow for his RoboDoc ranch. He frowned. 'Er, no,' he said. 'Absolutely not. You really shouldn't get your hopes up. I cannot stress enough how incredibly unlikely it is that…'

'Oh, don't worry about me,' I told him. 'I know the score, really. That's why I'm making the most of right now — this time when I can believe 100% that it's going to happen, because the big dream hasn't yet not come true.' Luke looked baffled, shook his head and went off to do complicated things with circuit boards and wiring while simultaneously trying to persuade venture capital firms to stump up the next round of funding for his amazing, arm-shaped robot.

What Luke didn't know then was that, by 2021, his brand new start-up would be worth more than 3 billion dollars. I sold all of my shares in July 2021, and that was the point at which my decision to invest the 35k would have been viewed as a brilliant choice by anyone who heard about it.

Here's the thing, though: it didn't become a brilliant choice only when it delivered a BPO; it was the right and best decision from the second I made it, because of how and why I made it.

My reasons for investing in Robodoc (which I dismissed as 'probably a bit ridiculous' at the time)

1) The Feel-Good Factor

Saying yes had a strong 'Feel-Good Factor' associated with it. I would have felt sad and disappointed if I'd said no. Why, you might be wondering, did it feel good to know that I was likely to lose 35k and be called a naïve, deluded fool by most people I knew? I couldn't have answered that question then but I can now: because (as you may remember from previous chapters) doing outrageous things that others might disapprove of lights me up. And because I'd made a Double Best choice. The Double Best Method is the only decision-making formula, as far as I'm aware, that allows you to feel good about, strive for and believe in your favourite of all the available options' BPOs for the maximum amount of time, *without giving a thought to the likeliness of that outcome if you don't want to.*

This is where Steps 6 and 7 of the Method — being who you want to be and acting in accordance with your Core Values — come into play. Some people might have 'financial caution' as a core value and feel so much better about themselves after deciding *not* to risk 35k on a highly precarious gamble — but I was not, and am not, one of those people.

Each of us has a Feel-Good response that is activated by different circumstances and actions — The Double Best Method enables you to choose the option that is most on the wavelength of your very own, personal Feel-Good requirements.

2) The Zone of Immense Possibility

Even if RoboDoc didn't work, I guessed that it would be at least two years before Luke said, 'That's it. It's all over.' That meant that I could spend two years firmly believing it would all work out brilliantly, and enjoying that belief: looking at ranches on Zillow, feeling excited, thinking and dreaming about huge success, imaginatively inhabiting a future scenario in which RoboDoc had conquered the world.

Those two years (or however long it might turn out to be) in The Zone of Immense Possibility, were a *guaranteed return on my investment.* The way I saw it, if I didn't invest, I wouldn't get to spend any time at all believing that I might one day be part of a billion-dollar success story. Whereas if I did, then, worst case scenario, I would be someone who had *nearly* been part of something completely amazing, which would also be a fun story to tell myself, though in a different way: 'I took a massive risk, knowing the odds were terrible, because I believed so hard and chose to back hope, not fear. Yes, I *am* a brave badass who isn't deterred by the prospect of failure.'

3) Is the worst outcome really that bad?

I didn't want to lose £35,000, but I knew it wouldn't be a disaster if I did. I would still be able to eat, pay my mortgage, take my family on holiday. (This is the crucial 'Is the worst case scenario really all that bad?' component of a Double Best analysis. If your answer to that question is, 'It's bad, yes, but not *that* bad' or 'It's terrible, obviously, but I'm willing to endure it if I have to,' then go ahead and choose your Double Best option — the one that gives you a shot at getting your favourite of all the BPOs. It doesn't matter if the odds are massively against success or that the the risk of the WPO is huge, *as long as you've decided in advance that you're willing to accept that WPO if that's the way things pan out.*)

4) Who I wanted to be

I wanted to help Luke, a really good person whom I liked a lot, and someone with immense talent and determination. I wanted to be optimistic rather than pessimistic, bold and daring, and not someone who allowed fear to persuade her that missing out on once-in-a-lifetime chances was a good idea. I did not want to be: sensible, cautious, realistic (ughhhhh — realistic is one of my least favourite words, and I've only just realised this; I noticed that I shuddered as I typed it), or timid. I wanted, in a big way, to be embarking upon a new adventure. Most of all — and this is crucial — I wanted to start becoming, via at first pretending to be, the person who invested in a risky start-up that turned out to be an astonishing success. Every time I told the story of my RoboDoc gamble to a new person, I made sure to say, 'Of course, there's no guarantee it's going to work out well,' but that wasn't what I was really thinking. Secretly, I was living the fantasy in my mind, and the great result was, as far as I was concerned, guaranteed. I just decided to allow myself to pretend. And the weird thing was, pretending kind of turned into becoming, and then being.

What do I mean by this, given that I didn't have any Robodoc profits in my bank account yet? How could I 'be' the person whose 35k gamble had paid off when it very much had not yet done so?

The answer is simple: by thinking and feeling as if the success was guaranteed, already in the bag. And in other ways too: by spending quite extravagantly while thinking, 'It's fine — RoboDoc millions are definitely on the way.'

This last part — the pretending and the acting-as-if — were the main things that convinced me I was probably being ridiculous, though I had no intention of stopping because I was having so much fun.

It wasn't until I discovered the worldview of Brooke Castillo that I realised my reasons were the opposite of ridiculous, and that the way I was thinking was not insane but actually quite sensible if I wanted to have the best possible experience of life and create the best possible results…

Chapter 5

The Double Best Method:
First Seeds

Here are some things Brooke Castillo says, often and powerfully, both on her podcast and in her Self-Coaching Scholars programme.

- Circumstances and events, things that happen, things other people say and do… None of these create our feelings. *Only* our thoughts and beliefs are capable of creating emotion inside us. So: fraudster Bernie Madoff's clients did not feel wealthy because they *were* wealthy. That was no longer their financial reality; Madoff had stolen and squandered their millions. Yet they still *felt* wealthy, because they were fooled by Madoff's lies. Their belief was: 'Lovely Bernie is taking super good care of my money and growing it for me. I'm richer than I've ever been.'

So, by believing 'Robodoc is destined for unparalleled success' before Luke had even registered his new business at Companies House, I created the same mental and emotional experience for myself that I would have had if it had already succeeded.

- Whenever we want a particular thing or outcome, or want to avoid that thing or outcome, it's always for the same reason: because of how we imagine it will make us feel, or what we believe it will prevent us from feeling.

If the truly desired result — feeling brilliant, abundant and successful — is the reason we want the success, then three cheers for getting that amazing feeling before the success result arrives, simply by believing it will!

- Our thoughts create not only our emotions, but also our results. Who we are 'being' at any given time, according to Brooke, is located in our thoughts and feelings, which then cause us to behave in certain ways. What this means is that 'becoming/being' the person who has the outcome we want, at the level of thoughts and feelings, makes us far more likely to behave in a way that creates that outcome. If we believe 'The success of my project is 100% guaranteed', and feel happy and excited about that, then we will keep taking dynamic and strategic action towards securing that result that we 'know' is in our future. This is very different from what our actions might be if we were thinking 'This might not work' and feeling doubtful.

I didn't know, until I heard it from Brooke, that our brains hate to experience cognitive dissonance. They both gather and — importantly — get to work to create evidence that confirms the correctness of their deeply ingrained beliefs. My brain did exactly that.

After nearly eighteen months of trying to find his next financial backer, Luke reluctantly told me that he might soon reach the end of the road.

'No, there's still loads of road left,' I said, in the high-pitched voice of a zealot-fantasist. 'We could pitch a reality TV show. I could write a book. There are still hundreds of things we could try. Don't dare to give up!'

I contacted a wealthy friend of mine and arranged for him to have lunch with Luke and discuss the possibility of him investing in RoboDoc. When that didn't work out,

I considered who else I might approach. I switched from thinking 'Luke will find RoboDoc's next financial backer' to 'I must find RoboDoc's next financial backer.'

In the end, I didn't need to — a venture capital provider turned up at the perfect moment and invested the several million dollars that would enable RoboDoc to do its stuff for the next three or four years. From that point forward, everything went about as well as it possibly could have.

Without that investor, who knows what would have happened? One thing I do know, though, is that I would have pitched the TV show and/or written a book called RoboDoc: The Poor Robot In Need Of More Money *— and what if one or both of those had led to RoboDoc getting its next round of funding?*

- Believing, in relation to things that might or might not happen in the future, is a different kind of believing. When we believe or disbelieve things about the world as it presently is, we can offer evidence to back up our belief, or dispute the validity of the evidence, if it's something we don't believe. When we're thinking about possible future outcomes, it's different. We cannot know whether we will succeed, fail, be happy or be miserable in the future. We can't always decide exactly what we want and then ensure that we get it; unexpected things interfere with that, as do things we can't control. Future outcomes are therefore unknowable, because we are not in charge of absolutely everything that happens in the world. Whether we believe things will go well or go badly, we are wholly making it up. It's a delusion: either an optimistic one or a pessimistic one. And therefore…

- We might as well believe, with full optimistic-delusional strength, that things will go well, until the actual second that a fail result comes in. Contrary to what most people think, there is no downside to doing this. Believing in a brilliant future feels amazing and massively increases your chance of creating the very success and happiness you want. And when fail results arrive — as they invariably do from time to time — they barely make a dent in your optimism and belief. Why? Two reasons: a) because of how much the brain hates cognitive dissonance. It looks at a fail result and thinks, 'Hm, this doesn't vibe with my strong belief that success is guaranteed. I'd better go and find something else to focus on that does.' And before you know it, you're believing in the success of your next endeavour or strategy, and feeling great again. And b) because another thing the human brain absolutely adores is: feeling fantastic. One of the three main aims of the human survival brain is to seek pleasure. It is so pleasing, so dopamine-providing, to feel great about the amazing future success you fully believe in that your brain, once it has established this as a habit, will not want to give it up, and so will find any and every possible way to avoid doing so.

Long before I heard Brooke teaching this, I instinctively understood that a pessimistic outlook was neither 'realistic' (because we cannot know what the future holds) nor advisable. Believing that you can't and won't succeed, and that everything will be awful, in no way protects us from future pain. Rather, it guarantees that we will experience psychological and emotional pain right now. And if we continue to think, 'This won't work, I'm bound to fail, everything will go wrong,' on a regular basis then what we will do is a) look for evidence that everything is going wrong, while ignoring the equally prominent or sometimes more prominent evidence that it isn't, and b) embed those misery-and-defeat-creating beliefs in our minds ever more deeply, thus ensuring that we will feel bad and discouraged both now and in the long term. Pessimistic thinking is a creator of pain, not an insurance policy against it.

- The 'rightness' of a decision has nothing to do with the eventual outcome, which we cannot know when choosing. Liking our reasons for making the decision is what makes it right. And as long as we like our reasons, it remains forever the correct decision, and we never need to beat ourselves up about it. If we don't like the outcome, we simply get to make a new decision — again, for reasons we like. No regrets appropriate or necessary, ever.

I wanted to cheer when I first heard Brooke say this. It was in 2018, when the RoboDoc outcome was still unknown; the company seemed to be faring extremely well, but Luke reminded me regularly that success was still not in the bag and that companies worth millions could lose all their value overnight, especially when they were still at the stage of being funded by investment rather than by profits from their products or services.

Still, I was thrilled to hear Brooke say that liking our reasons is what makes for a great decision. I loved all of my RoboDoc reasons, and, by 2018, I had spent six years enjoying 'being' (thanks to my belief) the person who had RoboDoc success as a guaranteed result in her future. My brain's confirmation bias and aversion to cognitive dissonance were happy to view Brooke's philosophy of life as evidence that I was doing everything right, at least in relation to investing in start-ups.

$$$

Once I realised my way of thinking was officially endorsed by Brooke Castillo, who was not only a genius life coach (I'd watched hours of her coaching by this point) but also CEO of a multi-million-dollar business, I decided to re-classify my reasons for taking that 35k gamble and think of them as extremely wise and sensible rather than 'probably ridiculous'.

That was when I remembered the conversation I'd had with my dad in the sea in 1984, while on a family holiday. I had wanted to stay at the beach, and my dad was explaining why we couldn't. (All the grown-ups insisted that every afternoon had to be spent napping —

even if we weren't tired, and even though the beach was beautiful and the sun was shining and spending any time at all in a dark room was obviously absurd. This formative experience, which happened every single year that we stayed near this beach, probably explains why Freedom is one of my core values and why I have huge trouble believing that any good at all can come from decisions made by sensible people.

Anyway, back to 1984. Somehow, my futile attempt to persuade my father to agree to stay at the beach all day resulted in him bringing up the political philosopher John Rawls. I haven't read Rawls myself, so I can't comment on the accuracy of what my dad told me, but I remember clearly what he said: according to Rawls, one could make decisions in two ways: the Maximax way, or the Maximin way. Those are the two strange words I mentioned earlier, that probably don't appear in dictionaries. Side note: it seems that Rawls was not the originator of these words. That was a man called John Von Neumann.

I was intrigued. I asked my dad what Maximax and Maximin meant, hoping this might keep us at the beach a little longer.

He explained by telling me about the umbrella example. I've no idea if this was the example used by John Rawls or if my dad came up with it himself, but I am going to use it forever because I think it provides the perfect illustration of Maximax and Maximin thinking.

The Umbrella Example

You're going out for the day. You have five meetings in town, in five different locations, and you're going to be walking from each one to the next. The weather forecast has predicted that it might rain heavily, but it also might not. The chance of rain is 50%. You have to decide whether to take your umbrella with you. Your only umbrella is a long, tall one that cannot be folded up and put inside a handbag or rucksack.

You have two choices:

1)   Take your umbrella;

2)   Don't take your umbrella.

A Maxi**max** decision-maker would always make the decision that **allows for the Best Possible Best Outcome**. (I'm hoping you can clearly see the origins of the Double Best Method here. When I first introduced it as a tool in my Dream Author Coaching programme, I called it 'Maximax/Maximin', which was not an especially catchy title.)

A Maxi**min** decision-maker, by contrast, would always make the decision that **avoids the Worst Possible Worst Outcome**.

Let's see how this plays out with the Umbrella Example:

Choice 1: Take your umbrella

BEST POSSIBLE OUTCOME: it doesn't rain; you're carrying an umbrella around all day.

WORST POSSIBLE OUTCOME: it rains, but you're protected and kept dry by your umbrella as you go from one meeting to another.

Choice 2: Don't take an umbrella

BEST POSSIBLE OUTCOME: it's dry and sunny all day and you're not carrying an umbrella around.

WORST POSSIBLE OUTCOME: it rains hard, and you get soaked between meetings because you have no umbrella.

Can you work out, from what you've read so far, what a Maximax-inclined person and a Maximin-inclined person would do in the above situation and why they would do it?

All will be revealed in the next chapter.

Chapter 6

More Seeds, And Some False Leads

Maxers and Minsters

This is what we're going to call them from now on — for ease of reference, and because it sounds cute. Maxers are those who tend to use Maximax thinking when making decisions, whereas a Minster is more likely to apply the principle of Maximin in choice-making situations.

Let's look at what this means in relation to the Umbrella Example.

A Maxer will look at the two best outcomes and compare them. She will probably decide that the Best Possible Best Outcome is: it doesn't rain, and she's also not carrying an umbrella around all day — and that's her decision made! She'll leave her umbrella at home and hope that the Weather Gods are kind enough to make her wish for that Double Best result come true.

A Minster, on the other hand, will focus on the worst outcomes offered by each of the two options. In most people's estimation, the worst outcome would probably be: it rains hard and you get soaked because you have no umbrella. A Minster would think that only a fool would choose the option that allows the only really bad outcome to remain on the table as a possibility. Minsters would rather carry dry umbrellas around all day than risk getting soaked.

Of course, most people are neither Maxers nor Minsters 100% of the time — most of us will use both approaches in different situations, depending on how much we want X or fear Y — but what struck me when I thought about this in 2018, after listening to Brooke Castillo, is that I was as close to being a dedicated, evangelical Maxer as it was possible to be, and that I wanted to stay that way.

The difference between Maximax and Maximin decision-making is simple. What's more complex and intriguing is all the layers and angles to the Maximax/Maximin modality that can be found if we explore a little further — which is what we often end up doing when we start asking ourselves whether we'd go Maxer or Minster in relation to a particular decision.

These are some of the questions that came up for me — in relation to Maximax and Maximin choice-making in the Umbrella scenario and also in other specific, real situations — when I started developing what would eventually become The Double Best Method:

- Is the worst possible outcome all that bad, really?

- Do I want to reevaluate, and maybe change my mind about what's desirable and what's not?

- Is the best outcome possible here? What if it's highly unlikely? Even if I think it's impossible, might I still want to go for it, for some other reason?

- What if someone thinks they're a Maxer and *would* take the umbrella, because the best of all possible outcomes for them is: lovely sunny weather all day, and they don't mind carrying the umbrella. Maybe they welcome the opportunity to build up their arm muscles, and know they'll enjoy the thrill of thinking, 'If it does rain, I'm protected.'

These important questions and nuances notwithstanding, I knew that I was a Maxer through and through. I was so proud of my new Maxer identity that I banged on about it with great enthusiasm. One day, I told my husband about it. He frowned, and said, 'That's ridiculous. Maximax? That's a terrible way to make decisions.'

I grinned, quite ready to listen to him and then explain why he was completely wrong and a sadly deluded Minster. 'Tell me more,' I said confidently.

'It makes no sense to say you're a "Maxer" or that Maximax thinking is the best way to make every decision,' said my husband.

I decided to bring in the big guns to help my case. 'Brooke Castillo agrees with me,' I told him. 'She's definitely a Maxer like me. She says a great way to make a choice is to imagine that, whichever thing you choose, it goes absolutely brilliantly and succeeds. Which would you choose if you knew that the outcome of either choice was guaranteed to be great? *That's* your best option.'

'That's so dumb,' said my husband, who is not tactful.

'No, it's not.' I frowned. 'Why is it?'

'Okay, let's say you've got £20,000 pounds in a savings account,' he said. 'That's all you own in the world, and you've also got no income coming in. The decision you have to make is: should you spend that whole £20,000 on lottery tickets? The best possible outcome of doing that is: you win a hundred million pounds. According to Brooke and Maximax, you should absolutely do it. In fact, you definitely shouldn't, because the chance of you winning the lottery is almost zero, and so you'd just be chucking away your money for no good reason. And you wouldn't be able buy food or pay rent. Or —'

'You can stop,' I told him. 'I get it.'

I couldn't deny that he had made an excellent point.

'Okay, first things first,' I said. 'Brooke Castillo absolutely would not, in that scenario, encourage anyone to spend their last 20k on lottery tickets. Her 'If you knew either option would work brilliantly…' approach is not meant to cover *absolutely every* situation, and certainly not ones where the worst case scenario is so horrific that it's not even worth risking for a second. Brooke's method is more for choices like: which house should I buy? Should I write this book or that book? Would I prefer to go on a safari or scuba-diving? Should I start a new business venture or side-hustle, knowing there's a risk it might fail?'

'What's the point in having The Big Solution to decision-making problems if it doesn't cover all decisions?' said my husband.

My perfectionist streak agreed with him. If I couldn't use Maximax thinking or Brooke's 'If you knew for certain that either one would lead to joy and prosperity…' approach in absolutely every decision-making situation, then…was there, maybe, a different choice-making method that would work 100% of the time and in absolutely every case?

My conviction that the world (and, most of all, I) needed an infallible process led me to the next stage of Double-Best-Method creation. I invented a formula that I called 'A, B, Succeed, Fail' (I liked the nursery-rhyme feel of the name; it reminded me of Agatha Christie's *One, Two, Buckle My Shoe*).

The A, B, Succeed, Fail Formula

In any decision-making situation…

1. List all the options
2. Ask yourself: 'Via which of these would I most like to succeed or get an amazing outcome?'
3. Then ask yourself: 'Via which of these would I most like to fail (assuming I have to) or get a sub-optimal outcome?'
4. If you've chosen the same option for each of questions 2 and 3, then your decision is made. Your best option is the one you would most want to choose if you knew things would go amazingly well, *and* the one you'd most want to choose if you knew it wasn't going to work out well.

I loved A, B, Succeed, Fail at first. In particular, the step of choosing your favourite way to fail (since we always might) appealed to me; I thought it was the perfect blend of happy Maxer thinking and acceptance of the parts of life and the future that we can never control. I loved the implicit suggestion that failure doesn't have to be all doom and gloom; there are aspects of failure we can enjoy and be proud of, or learn and benefit from. These, of course, involve core values and being, or becoming, who we most want to be.

I tried out A, B, Succeed, Fail with members of my Dream Author Coaching programme. People loved it! Well, some people did, anyway: the ones who chose the same option for 'Most want to succeed this way' and 'Most want to fail this way'. They would email me and say, 'Clearly, I should choose Option B if I'd rather both succeed *and* fail by route B.'

Yes. Clearly they should. However — and I'm sure many of you have spotted the problem already — quite a few people emailed me to ask what they ought to do if they chose different options for questions 2 and 3. One person said, 'I'd rather succeed with Option A, because that's the thing I'd really love most, if I could make it work. But I'd rather fail with Option B, because it would be too painful to fail at Option A. If I'm going to fail, I'd rather it was at something I don't care about at all.'

I realised I'd made a silly assumption while creating the formula. I'd assumed everyone would, like me, prefer to fail while trying to make their top favourite dream come true, rather than preferring to fail doing something they don't much care about. It turned out that I was incorrect. Most people chose the same option for 'Prefer to succeed at' and 'Prefer to fail at', but a significant minority did not, and this bothered me. It meant that A, B, Succeed, Fail was not the foolproof decision-making method I was looking for.

But do not despair, dear reader — you already have the flawless and brilliant Double Best Method. I gave it to you in Chapter 1, remember? All is well. All is for the best, in fact, in this best of all possible worlds. (Important note: this belief is often described as 'Panglossian', after a character named Dr Pangloss from Voltaire's *Candide*. Dr Pangloss was intended by his creator to be a silly and naïve object of derision. Well, #IStandWithPangloss, I'm afraid. Bring on your derision; I won't budge.)

I did not give up after identifying the flaws in A, B, Succeed, Fail. Instead, I thought hard about everything I liked and didn't like about it. One of the things I didn't like, for instance, was that it seemed to give equal weight to questions 2 and 3, whereas I wanted a method that was heavily biased in favour of best outcomes, and choices most likely to lead to best outcomes. I wanted to devise a method that, in its emphasis, was 90% Maxi and only 10% Min at most; 90% Succeed and only 10% Fail. I wanted the perfect Panglossian decision-making method.

At this point, some of you are probably wondering: why did I bother? Why didn't I just say, 'Ah, well!', pour myself a glass of white wine, put my feet up and watch telly instead? Why did I think it was so important to create the perfect choice-making method that would work superbly in every situation?

Great questions, all. And the simple answer is: because this really matters. The inability to make excellent choices that we feel totally happy about, and never regret, is an energy-draining and misery-making problem afflicting a huge number of human beings.

It's time to look at why getting good at decision-making is so vital for our mental health and happiness, and how gravely wrong most people are in their thinking about what constitutes a right or wrong choice.

Chapter 7

Why Most Of Us Are Bad Decision-Makers

If we could see the whole of the future — if there were a way of looking forward along each decision-path and seeing exactly what would happen two or ten years from now if we made this or that choice — then we would all be excellent at choosing. We could simply look ahead at the outcome we'd get if we chose Option A, then do the same for Option B, and then pick whichever we preferred. After all, we would be able to see what emotional outcome we would get from each scenario, wouldn't we? We'd know for sure which route would lead to our greater prosperity and happiness.

We cannot ever predict every aspect of the future, however. I think this is a wonderful thing, and not at all a drawback. As the late, great poet CH Sisson wrote in his poem *Uncertainty*:

The future is the only thing
That makes for thought. The past is past.
It brought its presents, had its fling,
But what it flung could never last.

The future has not lasted yet
Even the second that it can
And so is good for any bet.
It is the guessing makes the man…

Spot on, CH. It is the guessing — our inability to predict future events with any degree of accuracy — that requires us to make tough choices, be more of who we want to be, and embody our Core Values more fully. Uncertainty is the making of us. A life in which we never had to take Double Best risks would be a dreary, suspense-free and personal-growth-free ordeal. Whereas trying hard to create your optimal outcome in the face of uncertainty is Maxer Paradise! Think of all the believing, and enjoying of that belief, that you get to do.

Is anyone not convinced? Maybe the impressively jolly Maxer poet Edgar Albert Guest can persuade you…

IT COULDN'T BE DONE

Somebody said that it couldn't be done
But he with a chuckle replied
That "maybe it couldn't," but he would be one
Who wouldn't say so till he'd tried.
So he buckled right in with the trace of a grin
On his face. If he worried he hid it.
He started to sing as he tackled the thing
That couldn't be done, and he did it!

Somebody scoffed: "Oh, you'll never do that;
At least no one ever has done it;"
But he took off his coat and he took off his hat
And the first thing we knew he'd begun it.
With a lift of his chin and a bit of a grin,
Without any doubting or quiddit,
He started to sing as he tackled the thing
That couldn't be done, and he did it.

There are thousands to tell you it cannot be done,
There are thousands to prophesy failure,
There are thousands to point out to you one by one,
The dangers that wait to assail you.

But just buckle in with a bit of a grin,
Just take off your coat and go to it;
Just start in to sing as you tackle the thing
That "cannot be done," and you'll do it.

This was a poet who clearly understood that one can still make brilliant decisions in the face of uncertainty.

Most of us, unfortunately, are unaware of this truth. I thought I had grasped it several years ago, but in fact did not fully understand it at a bone-deep level until a just a few weeks before I started to write this book.

What does not being good at decision-making mean?

Most people believe that, if we don't know what will happen as a result of our decision, then we cannot be sure if it's good or bad until we see what outcomes it yields.

It stands to reason, then, that we're generally terrified of choosing in all but the most low-stakes situations.

When we believe that we *cannot be sure at the time of deciding* whether the decision we're making is the right one or the wrong one, several things happen:

1) We delay and avoid deciding, and instead allow ourselves to be buffeted around by events and other people's choices. We disempower ourselves by not actively choose a direction and then pursuing it; instead we clog up our minds with endless rumination around unmade decisions. We stay in what Brooke Castillo calls 'decision debt', which is a huge energy drain that doesn't get us anywhere.

2) We fail to recognise when we have in fact made a great decision. We agonise beforehand, we agonise afterwards, we tell ourselves that our reasons for doing what we did are 'probably bonkers' and wistfully think, 'Ah, well,' as if we've done something that on some level is regrettable — when, all along, a Double-Best analysis would have shown us that we'd made the best possible choice and one that gets to remain Right and Best no matter what the outcome turns out to be.

3) We make bad decisions *as a direct result* of saying to ourselves, 'I don't know what this choice I'm about to make will lead to, and therefore I might be getting it horribly wrong. I might be about to pick an option that will lead to great disaster.' These beliefs plunge us into a state of fear, which leads to lots of second-guessing. We erode our confidence in ourselves as potentially great decision-makers, and then, in a state of massive self-doubt, we tend to: dismiss our own inner wisdom; make, unmake and remake each decision dozens of times; make decisions based on what our friends or family think is best; consult others endlessly and sometimes compulsively, but not know whose opinions to trust — which of course is a whole new playground for our fear and doubt to get busy in.

4) We cause ourselves unnecessary anxiety based on a false belief (that we can't know if a decision is good or bad until we see its outcome), which then makes it more likely we'll choose unwisely. Panic sets in and we feel as if we're trapped in a lethal game of Russian Roulette. When chronic self-doubt whips up a storm of anxiety inside us, our 'higher' brains

step down from active duty. If we are making important decisions while feeling terrified of all the possible worst case scenarios, it will be the more basic, survival-focused part of our brain that's in charge. This basic brain of ours is very determined to keep us safe, and might regard, for example, a 35k gamble as highly likely to lead to terrible disaster. Our survival brains are easily alarmed and ever ready to push the panic button. They are really not great at distinguishing between 'risk of dismemberment and death' and 'risk of not being able to go on a foreign holiday next year'. Decisions made when we're in basic-brain mode will tip the balance decisively towards not attempting anything bold or ambitious, in case we fail and that's painful for us. Weirdly, though, our survival brain is more than happy to choose in favour of carrying on in exactly the way we have been, even if we've been bored and miserable for years. To the survival brain, the familiar feels safe — probably because it knows we can survive the experience we've been having already for several decades.

5) We beat ourselves up mercilessly if a past decision leads to something happening in our lives that we don't like. We torture ourselves with regrets and tell ourselves we could and should have known, and done it differently. No, we couldn't. Because we didn't, right? And if we'd done it differently, some unforeseeable turn of events might have led to us being crushed to death by a hippopotamus falling from a great height as we sauntered down the street one day. How can we know for certain that would not have happened, if we'd chosen Option B instead of Option A? We can't, and therefore it makes no sense to believe everything would have been better if we'd made a different choice.

The simple truth is that we cannot make the best possible decisions until we are fully clear about what that means. It does not mean 'Making a choice that ends up leading to brilliant results that we love'. Why on earth would we want to make it mean that? It would be as foolish as telling ourselves that deciding to go to sleep when we're exhausted cannot be regarded as a sound decision unless we know for certain that, on this particular night, our neighbour won't break into our house, steal all our treasured possessions and punch our beloved poodle on the nose. If he did all of those things, would that make our decision to go to sleep when we were tired wrong or foolish? Of course not — we could not possibly have known.

What second-guessing looks like in decision-making

I recently attended a series of online events delivered by life coach Kara Loewentheil, and was fascinated to hear her say 'Second-guessing causes us to ignore red flags, to go along with things that don't feel right, and to be disconnected from our values.' Exactly. Kara, whose coaching has a specific emphasis on feminism, mentioned several times in her presentations that second guessing is something most women do. She's right — and a quick Twitter poll I ran revealed that 58% of men also second-guess and agonise either before or after most decisions. The percentage of women who said they did was 59%.

We know we're second-guessing when we ask ourselves the following four questions and do not allow ourselves to answer them promptly and decisively:

1) **What if I'm wrong in my principle?** Example: I'm thinking of breaking up with Joe because he has lied to me once, and I don't think lying is ever acceptable. *Thought-loop: 'But he's so sorry and he's promised never to do it again. But I don't think it's okay that he's done it*

once. But I should forgive him, surely. But I really don't think it's forgivable. Is it? Am I wrong about this?'

2) **What if I'm wrong in my perception?** Example: I'm thinking of breaking up with Mandy because she doesn't care about me. *Thought-loop: 'But maybe she does. Not wanting to watch every single movie I want to watch doesn't necessarily mean she doesn't care about me. But if she cared, she would totally watch war films with me. Any loving partner would. But is that even true? Maybe she loves me but just dislikes war films? How can I know? I could ask her, but how could I trust her answer?'*

3) **What if it turns out badly?** Example: I've written a play and I want to stage it in my converted barn annexe, but I probably won't because it might go horribly wrong. *Thought-loop: 'What if no one buys a ticket, and I have to tell everyone it's cancelled because no one was interested? That would be so humiliating. I can't risk that. But it might go well! And it can't go well if I don't do it. But it might be a shameful disaster. How can I know if tickets would sell, and if everyone would enjoy it?'*

4) **What if I end up hating myself for getting it wrong?** Example: I'm considering standing up for someone

who's getting trashed and cancelled on social media, but last time I did that, I did it in a rash, hot-headed way and inadvertently made the fighting worse, not better. *Thought loop: 'I should definitely keep out of this one. That other time, I made it so much worse. What an idiot I was! Ugh. I hate myself for doing that. Seriously, only a complete numbskull could mess up so badly. But I want to stick up for this person who's being unfairly vilified online. Yeah, but remember how shit you were at doing that before? Right, but does that mean I should never try again?'*

Some of the beliefs that lead to doubting and second-guessing our every decision are:

1) I can't/don't trust myself (to know what's right, to stick to my plan, to make it work, to desist from launching a savage self-criticism campaign if it doesn't go well).

2) I'm not important, clever or deserving enough to make decisions, or to get what I truly want. Who am I to want things anyway?

3) I can't be the authority figure here. That's just impossible. Surely there must be a bigger authority who can tell me what to do?

Sure, there are experts in various subjects, and we can and should absolutely consult them when necessary. But there is no bigger authority than you on the question of: what is the right thing for *you* to do in any particular situation? Only you know what you desire, which values you want to believe in and embody, what you're willing to risk, who you want to be, and the why of all of these.

The great news, for anyone who believes rightness and certainty are necessary in order to make great decisions, is that we can be both right and certain…

Chapter 8

How To Be Right And Certain

I t's vital that we train ourselves to be not merely good at deciding but incredible at it — because it is via decisions, and the action that follows from them, that we create the results and the lives we want. As discussed in the previous chapter, it's hard to feel resolved and enthusiastic about anything when you're afraid you're going to get it wrong and thinking things like, 'There's so much uncertainty surrounding this choice.' If only we could know we were right and feel completely certain in each choice we make...

Well, the twist here (and, as a writer of mystery novels, I do love a good twist!) is that we can. Let's examine the following two pieces of excellent news:

1. We can be right when making decisions

A right or good or best decision is one that's made in the right way, and for the best reasons — ones we thoroughly approve of. Many people make some of their decisions in this way without The Double Best Method. Using The Double Best Method is the way to ensure that you always do it.

One of the much-vaunted pieces of wisdom in the life-coaching world is that there are no wrong decisions. I disagree. Though there is some truth to the idea ('We are always either winning or learning,' as Brooke Castillo says), I believe there are many suboptimal ways to make a choice, and many deeply flawed deciding-adjacent practices that we can and must learn to avoid — for example, downing a bottle of vodka and then doing precisely what your cousin Dave thinks you should do without first asking yourself if you agree with him. That is a decision-making process that I'm happy to call wrong. So is not doing something because you're too scared, without first questioning if there's anything to fear. Or choosing based on a thought error of the 'Jasper forgot my birthday and must therefore hate me' variety. Or making a decision with a threat to yourself built-in:

'Listen, Sonny Jim — if this goes tits-up, I'm never going to let you live it down. I'm going to be in your brain taunting you about it forever.'

We can make decisions that are right by:

1) Checking that we're not believing anything about decision-making or the particular circumstances that might not be true;

2) Liking our reasons for making the choice;

3) Liking who we're being, or moving closer to becoming, by making the choice;

4) Liking all the things we *can* be certain about when we make the choice, and preferring them to the things we could be certain about if we chose a different option.

2. We can be certain when making decisions

Can we be certain of the exact outcome our choice will create? No. But we can be sure of many things, nonetheless: our preferences, our thoughts about risk, our fears, our principles and values, and who we want to be or become.

When you think about it, that's a huge amount of stuff for a person to be sure of. Each time we ask ourselves a question like 'How can I possibly choose in the face of so much uncertainty?', we're failing to question our implicit assumption. There isn't necessarily *so much* uncertainty, there is simply *some* uncertainty. And we can immediately bring in far more certainty, in all of the areas described in the above paragraph.

When we accept that some of our best and right decisions will inevitably lead to outcomes we're not so keen on (because we can never control the whole world and other people), and that this will never mean our decision was 'the wrong one' or 'a stupid mistake', then we can finally kiss goodbye to regret forever. The rightness of choices resides in how and why we make them, not in what they lead to. And we can be certain about the truth and wisdom of this, because nothing else makes sense or is feasible.

The Truth About Outcomes

Most people give themselves a very hard time when a choice they make creates any sort of situation they don't like. Even when the unwanted component of a result is only a tiny detail, and most of the result is great, we can still beat ourselves up in this way — because that tiny detail must be our fault, right? After all, we were the ones who chose in the way we did.

In 2010, I moved my family from West Yorkshire to Cambridge. There was no reason to do this other than that I desperately wanted to. Previously, I had lived in Cambridge for two years, between 1997 and 1999, and it was my favourite place in the world.

So in February 2010 we left Yorkshire behind and bought a house in Cambridge that I can *now* see is beautiful and absolutely perfect for us in every way. It took me just over a decade to realise this fully, however. For about a year after we first moved in, I obsessed over every tiny detail that was not perfect. I couldn't understand why at the time, but now I see it clearly: I had an irrational belief that 'Something must be wrong', because I had randomly and recklessly (as my fear-brain saw it) moved my family across the country for no good reason other than desire and preference. At the time, I was unaware that those are the very best reasons, always, for doing anything.

My buying-a-house-in-Cambridge experience could not have been more different from the experience I'd had in 2006, when I moved from Bingley in West Yorkshire to Utley, about ten minutes down the road. On that occasion, the move was, as I saw it, 'a necessity'. My two children were two and three years old, and we were living in a house with no outside space apart from a small balcony. The kids' bedrooms were tiny too. My husband and I agreed that we 'had to' move. (This, of course, was not true, but we believed it was.) As a result, I adored the house we bought in Utley from the second I set foot in it. It was easy for me to do so, because in my mind, necessity and duty (to give my children decent-sized bedrooms and a garden) had been in charge of that move, not me. I'd really had no choice, I told myself. If anything were to go wrong, therefore, it would not be my fault. And the new Yorkshire house had been an absolute bargain — seven bedrooms, heaps of character and history, beautiful gardens, and we'd got it for £310,000. When I first saw that price on the Rightmove website, I thought it was a typo.

In contrast, the Cambridge house we bought in 2010 cost £685,000. I wasn't at all sure we'd be able to afford to stay in it forever, which brought both money worries and having-to-sell-my-home-after-I've-grown-attached-to-it worries into the picture.

Like the Utley house, our new Cambridge house had plenty of character and history. It too was beautiful, if a little shabby around the edges. But this time, fear tainted my perception of everything. This time it was all down to me; necessity and duty were not running the show. A wrong decision would be *absolutely my fault*; my wants had been the driving force behind the 'uprooting of our lives', as I often fearfully thought of it.

In the run-up to the move, I had a horrible recurring nightmare in which only the houses and people were different each time. The dream always had the same plot-line: we sold our house, bought a new one which seemed ideal at first, and then suddenly found out that there was something wrong with our new house — chillingly wrong; there was a definite horror movie vibe to this dream. Whatever was wrong, we knew it could never be fixed. I would run back to my old house, crying, and always in the middle of the night, and beg its new owners to sell it back to us — for double what they'd paid for it, if that was what it would take. In each recurrence of the dream, our buyers solemnly shook their heads and said, 'Sorry, but no. It's too late. It's our house now.'

It's hardly surprising, given that I was anxious about money and haunted by horror dreams of mistaken house moves, that I moved to Cambridge and soon found myself bursting into tears if I spotted a cigarette butt on the pavement outside my new home, or if a car alarm went off in the night. I was terrified by anything that my frightened brain could construe as evidence that this choice, for which I felt solely responsible, might have produced any negative outcomes at all.

A similar thing happened to one of the writers in my Dream Author Coaching programme recently. She got an offer of representation from the literary agent of her dreams — an undisputed superpower in the publishing industry — and at the same time she got offers from two other agents, both with very good reputations. She knew that in order to say yes to her dream agent, she would have to say no to the other two. The thought 'I am about to turn down really great offers from two very good, reputable agents', was followed closely by 'Who do I think I am? Do I really think I'm at the level of this Uber-agent superstar? Am I getting ideas above my station?'

These thoughts triggered a fear response in her. She said yes to her dream agent, and then immediately started looking for evidence that she'd done the wrong thing. She emailed me in a panic, saying she'd 'just found out' that Writer X had not had a good experience with that agent, and Publisher Y had warned her that the Uber-agent was too famous and busy to pay her any attention, and might palm her off on a junior colleague before too long.

I pointed out that there is not a single literary agent in the world with whom no writer has ever had a bad experience. I asked her how she'd be feeling if she'd said no to the agent of her dreams, and yes to one of the other two. 'Oh, I'd be even more convinced I'd made the wrong decision,' she said quickly. 'I'd be thinking, "I must be the world's biggest fool, turning down such an incredible offer from the agent I'd most love to work with."'

Exactly. And I'd have felt worse and been convinced I'd made the wrong choice if, instead of moving to Cambridge in 2010, I'd told myself that I should count my blessings and stay put in West Yorkshire, when I knew for certain that wasn't what I wanted most.

Here's the thing: very often, we get the outcome we want and discover there's *something else that comes with it that we don't want*. When we made our choice, we thought only about the wanted part of the outcome, and not what its byproducts might be. We did not know what precise thoughts and feelings it would produce in us, so when we find ourselves experiencing those thoughts and feelings, it can be a shock. 'I didn't choose this!' we say to ourselves, and it's very easy to move swiftly from there to, 'I must have made a terrible mistake.'

Happily, this isn't true. What is true is that — to bring in another of Brooke Castillo's wise sayings — 'There' (wherever we will land once we choose our preferred option and move towards it) is never better than 'Here' (our current situation). It's different, and some of the problems we have Here will disappear once we get There, but we will also, for sure, encounter new problems There that we do not currently have Here. Different upsides and different downsides are attached to every circumstance that might find ourselves in. And of course, we are always fully aware of the downsides of Here, because we're in it. It's crucial to remember, therefore, that when we choose There because we're attracted by the upsides it offers, we must take into account that there will also and inevitably be downsides that come with it.

To be clear: I'm not thinking only of Worst Possible Outcomes here, though they are included in the category of downsides; I'm also talking about the regular, undramatic and prosaic downsides that pertain to every choice we make. We must be careful not to make these mean that we've made the wrong decision, just because we don't love every single micro-result in our new, There-ish set of results.

Instead of rushing to label our choice as 'wrong' whenever we notice a downside in our newly chosen circumstance (occasional cigarette butts on the street outside our house, for instance), we can and should say to ourselves, 'Wait, would I prefer to go back to the downsides I had before, in my old situation?' This often neatly reveals that, actually, what we were secretly hoping for was 100% Flawless Perfection, which I'm afraid is rarely an option on the Choices Menu.

One of the things I love about The Double Best Method is that it encourages you to think positively and in advance about downsides as well as upsides. In my Double Best calculations, I regularly say to myself, 'Yes, I'm happy to take the risk of this negative result and here's why...' The whole Double Best framework is set up to reveal to us that, very often, downsides are a) nothing to worry about; just a regular part of life, and b) so, so worth it.

Here are some great reasons to choose a particular downside:

- We prefer it to the downside that any other choice would give us;

- We only give ourselves the chance of an amazing, Double Best outcome if we accept this downside;

- Many if not most downsides, on closer inspection, turn out to be not that bad at all and we judge that this is one of those;

- We love our reasons for choosing the option with this downside;

- We love the story we get to tell if we choose the option with this downside;

- We love who we get to be, or who we move closer to becoming, by selecting the option that has this downside attached to it.

Don't be fooled by feelings

It's important to remind ourselves regularly that a real, powerful, deeply felt emotion *does not prove the presence of a valid or true thought*. Many people often get confused and believe that it does. I do it myself. It's easy to fall into the trap of thinking, 'If I feel this bad, someone must have done something wrong, or something terrible must have happened.'

Nope. It's simply not true. If I feel furious and betrayed because my friend Jill has invited me to her fancy-dress party and I loathe fancy-dress, then I'm probably thinking something like, 'How could she do this to me? She obviously doesn't care about me at all and has done this just to spite me.' If I'm believing those thoughts, then the torrent of betrayal feelings inside me will be very real and might even result in unpleasant physical symptoms. This does not make my thoughts about Jill's betrayal true. In fact, they are nonsense. Jill is allowed to have whatever kind of party she wants, and if I hate fancy dress, I can either not attend and explain why, or ask Jill for special permission to turn up in my normal attire of jeans and a shirt. I needn't take it personally and get upset.

We should all be thrilled to learn that emotions can be real while the thoughts creating them are false. There is so much freedom for us in this knowledge. It means that when we find ourselves feeling scared and full of doubt after making a big decision that's going to take us well out of our comfort zone, we can say to ourselves, 'This fear doesn't mean I made the wrong choice, and neither does my recurring thought of "You've probably ****ed it all up, you nincompoop!" Even though these unpleasant feelings are real, the thoughts causing them are trying to trick me. They're simply not true.' This immediately allows us to put some distance between us and the problem thoughts, and decreases their power over us.

Sometimes we are going to feel terrible for a while after making the perfect choice. Some Double Best choices require us to make sacrifices, be brave and do difficult things. That doesn't make them wrong.

Chapter 9

The Double Best Method Is Born

Some of you might be wondering: so when was The Double Best Method finally created? What happened after Maximax/Maximin and A, B, Succeed, Fail were judged and found wanting? Did The Double Best Method just magically appear at that point?

No. I formulated the Double Best Method when I asked myself, 'How can I take all the decision-making wisdom I've gathered so far and turn it into the simplest, quickest-to-explain process imaginable?'

Is The Double Best Method really quick to explain, if I feel the need to write a whole book about it? Yes. This book contains the very quick and simple method plus lots more extra goodies. Who doesn't want extra goodies, right?!

Here's the short version of The Double Best Method, for anyone who wants or needs to elevator-pitch it: you choose the option that gives you the chance of getting your favourite of all the possible outcomes, as long as the worst possible outcome attached to that option isn't a deal-breaker.

When I thought about the drawbacks associated with both Maximax/Maximin and A, B, Succeed, Fail, I realised that both give exactly the same weight and consideration to the positive as to the negative. Ideologically, this did not work for me. I wanted the perfect decision-making process to be massively slanted in favour of the positive — partly because then, if The Double Best Method really catches on globally, millions more people will end up creating their ideal outcomes, which will lead to a happier and more fulfilled world. And also because, let's face it, most of the fears that prevent us from really going for it and trying to achieve our dream results are absolutely not, or should not be, good enough reasons to deter us. Generally, the Worst Possible Outcome we fear isn't getting chewed to death by a crocodile; it's overwhelmingly more likely to be

'Someone disapproves of me a bit' or 'I have to have a difficult conversation with my spouse/friend/sister.'

The way the Double Best Method is presented — those particular steps in that particular order — first invites us to think about what we truly want, and to recognise that this choice might be the first step towards getting it. Then it effectively says to us, 'And is there really any potential downside that you want to allow to prevent you from pursuing this amazingness?' I just love how biased in favour of the positive it is! I also love that it contains a checks-and-balances stage, for anyone with Minster inclinations, or who has only 20k in their bank account and is considering spending every last penny of it on lottery tickets.

How and why using the The Double Best Method turns you into a decision-making genius

Throughout this book, I've described The Double Best Method variously as a process, a formula and a method. It's all of these. At this point in our journey, I feel like calling it a recipe as well — and you don't even need to go to the supermarket to find the ingredients. They're all inside you already — super convenient, right? Just follow the step-by-step recipe and you will end up with the perfect dish: a brilliant, best and right decision (which means brilliant, best and right for you *and only you*, now, not correct for everybody at all times in world history. There is no such thing as a universally correct decision because we all want, and don't want, different outcomes. We all have different Core Values.)

In order to benefit from the full magic of The Double Best Method, you will need to understand four crucial things:

1) The policy works *always*, and therefore you should *always* follow it. You might be tempted, sometimes, to think, 'No, it doesn't apply here' or 'This is a unique situation in which The Double Best Method just won't work.' Thankfully, the Double Best Method always works. Highly educated and sophisticated thinkers are unaccustomed to following formulas when it comes to making important decisions in their lives; they are extremely susceptible to believing that each new choice-making scenario is unique and deserving of a nuanced and individual approach. Here's the thing,

sophisticated doubters: the very individuality and nuance you crave *is a built-in and prominent feature* of The Double Best Method. When answering questions like 'Which is my favourite of all of these Best Possible Outcomes?', you will have to ask yourself *why* you want this, or don't want that, and what this means about you, and whether you want to continue to be someone who values this and does not value that. So resist the temptation to believe there's anything restrictive, formulaic or reductive about The Double Best Method. All the freedom you want is right there in the process, between the lines of the step-by-step recipe. Those steps require you to find the nuance and dive deep into the many layers of an issue in order to come up with your Double Best answers.

2) A decision-making genius is clever enough not to fall for an untrue thought like: 'A decision-making genius wouldn't/shouldn't need a formula in order to make her best possible choices'. On the contrary, having an infallible formula is the magic asset that no decision-making genius wants to be without. Why? Well, the obvious answers are a) because the

Double Best recipe works in all situations. That's true; it does, and so why wouldn't anybody want to avail themselves of it? And b) a blanket policy, to be applied in all choice-making scenarios, saves you effort and energy. You don't have to waste time asking yourself, 'How should I go about making this decision? Maybe I should ask my friend Carol what she thinks. Or maybe for this one I should just list as many pros and cons as I can think of, and then award points for pros and minus points for cons...' All your mental effort, if you're following The Double Best Method, will be expended on the substance of the choice, because a reliable policy eliminates that layer of 'How shall I approach the making of this decision?'

3) A decision-making genius recognises that if we have a plan for how we're going to make decisions *in advance of*, and in preparation for, finding ourselves in a real, live and possibly high-stakes decision-making situation, then we get to think and plan with our calm and wise higher brains about the best way to make choices, long before the emotional confusion of our survival brain in a 'Help! I don't

know what to choose!' panic is upon us. Whenever our basic brain is freaking out because we've been given some kind of ultimatum ('Who do you want to marry? Prince William or Lady Gaga? You have twenty-four hours to decide.'), we can refer back to the strategy endorsed by our higher brain and immediately have the comfort of a solid container for our confused emotions. We might still be thinking, 'I don't know what to do', but we will also think, 'I know exactly what to do when I don't know what to do.' One of the most brilliant things about The Double Best Method is that, once you know it, you will always know what to do *structurally*. And following the formal steps of the process will soon reveal to you what you want to do in relation to the content of each choice.

4) Whenever we believe that we know what to do *at any level at all* (as in our above thought of 'I know exactly what to do when I don't know what to do'), it enables us to gain confidence in our agency and effectiveness, and to move forward. If we follow The Double Best Method, we can't help but notice ourselves taking steps in the direction of deciding

brilliantly — because we're following the Deciding Brilliantly Recipe! We get to witness ourselves doing this, and we see that taking decisive action is now in our repertoire. This builds up our trust in our own ability to create great results in our lives.

And those are not The Double Best Method's only star qualities. If you want to know what else I love about this brilliant decision-making recipe, then read on…

Chapter 10

The Top Ten Benefits Of The Double Best Method

Here are the Top Ten things the Double Best Method has going for it:

1) It allows us to make decisions based on certainty, that are definitely right, and that will remain right no matter what…

…because we only ever need to be certain about ourselves — what we want, prefer and judge to be serious enough that it ought to deter us. There's no requirement to be right about, or certain of, future outcomes. All we need to know for certain, and be right about, is what we want, think and choose in the present moment.

2) It produces bespoke, personal decisions.

One person's best case scenario is another's complete and utter fiasco. The Double Best Method works equally well for every one of us and guides us towards the absolute best decision for us and us alone. How does it do this? By making our opinion the only one that it takes into account. Look back at the descriptions of the steps in Chapter 1. It's *your* opinion of what's the best of the various Best Possible Outcomes that the Method asks for, not your Aunt Gertrude's. It's *you* who are being asked,' Is the chance of the Double Best result worth the risk of the Worst Possible Outcome?', not your hair stylist or your optician.

The prioritising of your preferences and values and the absolute irrelevance of anybody else's helps to build trust in your own judgement and to reinforce the very important principle that what you want and think really matters. You cannot help but receive this message loud and clear when you use The Double Best Method. Soon you find that self-trust is building inside you and you're starting to treat your intuitions, gut instincts and inner wisdom with the massive respect they deserve.

3) It promotes a realistic assessment of what we can and can't control.

The serious consideration of possible outcomes, both best and worst, subliminally encourages us a) to try to exert our agency wherever we have the power to do so, and b) to stop trying to control what we can't, like the future and what other people might do or not do that we cannot possibly predict, and/or what we might end up thinking about the results of this decision three years from now, depending on what other people do or don't do. The Double Best Method keeps us at the highest end of our personal power spectrum, by locating the rightness of our choices in the known, and in the parts of the outcome-creation process of which we are in sole charge.

4) No statistical analyses or assessments of odds are needed in order for it to work brilliantly.

Notice that the Method asks us to consider our favourite and least favourite potential outcomes without requiring us take a view about how likely or unlikely these are. Nor does it ask us to make decisions strategically in order to maximise the chance of getting our best possible outcome. Most of the literature on decision-making so far (the field of game theory, and the Prisoner's Dilemma, to cite just two examples) has been entirely focused on strategic thinking — on how best to increase the likelihood that you will get a good result, with the definition of 'good result' here being 'things work out well for you'.

The problem with this approach is that, if our carefully- and strategically-made choice leads to an outcome we dislike, or not the precise one we were shooting for, then we're likely to regard our decision as a fail. When we make Double Best choices, on the other hand, we cannot fail in that same way. Although there might be new, different decisions to make in the future if we don't like a particular outcome, there will be absolutely no need, ever, to torment ourselves with regrets. All of the rightness and greatness of our decisions will be fully realised *in the moment of making them*. No matter whatever happens afterwards, it cannot render our decision incorrect in retrospect. This, surely, is the only sane, encouraging, empowering and compassionate approach to choice-making.

5) It is supremely flexible.

The Double Best Method allows you to prioritise different things in different situations. Whenever you want to, you can let boldness or outrageous ambition be the most prominent 'note' in your decision-making. Equally, if you're keen to be extra cautious after a bumpy phase in your life and you feel drawn to playing it safe, The Double Best Method allows for that too.

It's the use of the words 'favourite' and 'best' in the Method's steps that is key here. Those words can mean whatever we want to make them mean. They *always* mean 'the item, or outcome, that is preferable to me now, for whatever reason feels most persuasive in this moment.' If you want to get all statistical and strategic and make 'best' mean 'most likely to succeed according to the findings of past surveys and my opinion about how I might influence the actions of others', then you absolutely can. Or, you can choose without so much as a glance in the direction of likely outcomes and without a thought for what anyone else might think or do in response to your decision.

If you're feeling particularly noble and want to be the bigger and better person, then you can decide to send flowers to your friend who has broken her ankle, even though she kicked your dog two weeks ago when she was in a bad mood. This might well be the choice that gives you your favourite of the Best Possible Outcomes, if your Core Values of compassion and empathy are in the ascendant that day. Equally, if you are in more of a 'consequences for bad guys' mood when deciding, then the very same super-flexible decision-making method will lead to you deciding not to send flowers, but to send instead a sharp note about ankle-related karma for dog-kickers.

The Double Best Method allows you to prioritise desire in one scenario ('I love Prince William! Nothing matters to me but that! *Nothing*!) and principle in another ('I don't care how delicious it is — I'm not buying coffee from a company that locks its employees in the cellar with rats and spiders if they're a minute late for work.').

As well as being flexible itself in the above-described way, it also encourages flexibility in us. The questions we ask ourselves during the Double Best process often bring to light concerns, fears and cravings we did not know we had. I've been using the Method regularly for some time now, and I've noticed that it's caused me to develop a new willingness to go on a journey of discovery with each decision I make; I might start out thinking I know exactly what I want to achieve and avoid, but when I consider the Double Best questions seriously, I almost always find that something quite new and unexpected emerges. I've switched over from being a decider who starts out thinking she knows what she wants and fears and then tries to choose in order to get or avoid getting those things, to being a decider who assumes she will only truly discover what she wants, thinks and fears once she embarks upon the decision making journey.

I see this same thing happen with my coachees, friends and family. A friend of mine started out believing that the Worst Possible Outcome she feared most was her mother's disapproval, or conflict with her mother, if she chose a particular course of action. A Double Best analysis revealed that in fact it wasn't merely disapproval or a row that she was scared of — she could have handled that, no problem. Her true and deep fear was that *she would lose her mother altogether* — that her making a particular choice would result in their relationship ending for ever.

A family member of mine went through all the Double Best steps, and once they had led her to what we both thought was her Double Best Choice, she said, 'I don't like this Method. It's annoying.'

'Tell me more,' I said, pen in hand.

'It annoys me that my Double Best Choice is *that,*' she said contemptuously. 'It shouldn't be that. The fact that it is means I'm a dick.'

Further discussion revealed that, although she yearned for a particular thing, she believed she was weak and a doormat for wanting it. This, of course, necessitated a new Double Best Choice, because clearly there was a significant clash between a scenario she very much wanted to choose in favour of, all other things being equal (which they never are), and the who-she-wanted-to-be/Core-Values part of the picture.

6) It understands that possibility, not the realisation of possibility, is where the true magic lies.

When we choose the option that might — only might, with no guarantees — give us our favourite of all possible outcomes, we reinforce in ourselves the important principle that trying to create the result we most want in the face of uncertainty and possible failure is a hugely valuable thing to do. When we pursue, happily and with belief, goals that seem uncertain or even impossible, we stretch ourselves, reside in optimistic belief for longer (which is a wonderful place to be if we want to establish fantastic-feeling thought habits), develop new skills and often end up achieving what we previously believed was impossible. Even if we don't end up creating our dream scenario, we will certainly produce better results than we would have if we had aimed lower or 'more realistically', as some people would say. (Minsters, mainly.)

I am convinced that hoping for, working towards and believing in the possibility of our heart's truest desire is the best thing any human being can do. The Double Best Method implicitly suggests to us, every time we use it, that the aim of each decision we make should be to keep open the possibility of our favourite result for as long as we can.

That possibility and potential is rightly treated as an end in itself — if we've chosen our favourite possibility then we have chosen well, according to the Method. This is a crucial part of the genius of Double Best choice-making, because in fact (and you might want to argue with me about this, which is fine) the possibility, and the moving towards, and the believing and feeling great in advance of the result coming in, and knowing it might never arrive...all of this *is itself the best result of all.*

Who doesn't believe me about that last point? Have you ever had something really exciting happen, and then weeks or months pass and the thing starts to feel less and less exhilarating and mind-blowing, and soon you're used to it and thinking of it as just part of regular life? And then you start planning your next endeavour that might or might not succeed? And the adrenaline starts to flow again, and you're stretching your capabilities and requiring bold action of yourself again...

Uncertainty and possibility are the making of us. They're the most fun thing, and where all the suspense lies. By comparison, getting exactly what you want every time, guaranteed, is…well, it's a bit dull. The Double Best Method centres the amazingness of possibility in its calculations. It casts the chance of a great result in the leading role, and cuts the ties that, in some people's minds, bind good decision-making to actual outcomes that result from decisions.

7) It encourages us to consider seriously that the worst case scenario we fear might not be all that bad, or indeed bad at all.

This is a quick and easy one: the question 'Is the risk of the Worst Possible Outcome worth taking in order to stand a chance of getting my Best Possible Outcome?' is almost begging for the answer 'Yes, actually, it is.' We know, by the time we reach this point in the Method, that if we could only decide the risk *is* worth taking, then our very favourite possibility will open up to us. We are therefore suitably incentivised to answer that question in the affirmative — which is great, because most of the WPOs we fear are really not that bad at all. I have, in the past, shut off the possibility of my very favourite outcome because I feared a WPO like, 'X will be annoyed at having to rearrange something that's already in her diary.'

8) It helps us to avoid catastrophising, lose-lose decision-making.

Some people — Minsters in particular — can quite easily forget about potential upsides altogether when making decisions. Their train of thought might go like this: 'If I choose X, then my family will hate me. But if I choose Y then my colleagues will hate me. Either way, I'll be an object of loathing. There's nothing I can do here that will prevent that…'

Notice how no thought at all is being given to the good results that doing X or Y might yield! The Double Best Method reminds us very cheerfully that every option has a BPO attached to it as well as a WPO, and, as I've already said above, it subtly directs us to pay more attention to the positive than to the negative. Apart from anything else, its name does this very powerfully.

9) It ensures that our higher brain always contributes significantly to each decision we make.

I've covered this already, but it's worth repeating: by following a policy that our higher, wiser brain has devised with our best interests firmly in mind, we ensure that, however emotional and hot-headed we might be feeling — however caught up in neurotic, survival-brain drama — we have a solid structure to lean on. Fortunately, this structure requires us to sit down with a pen and paper, think seriously and then answer a series of quite taxing questions. By the time we've performed the process from start to finish, we cannot help but be in a calmer and more balanced frame of mind. And if we're overly emotional, we might not even be able to answer the questions at first — we're likely to think to ourselves, 'I can't do this Double Best analysis now. I need to weep and drink wine for a bit.' This is actually brilliant; it's the Double Best Method's way of putting the brakes on and stopping you from deciding too rashly while you're still in an emotionally triggered condition.

10) It doesn't require you to be nobler, braver or more virtuous in any way than you currently are, or want to be.

This could have been a sub-clause of item 8 on the list, because it relates to flexibility, but I decided it deserved a listing in its own right. A crucial and wildly neglected component of self-care is giving yourself a break from time to time from the idea that you should be constantly improving yourself. *Don't Change A Thing.*

The Double Best Method is wholly non-judgemental as a framework. It works brilliantly for Actual You, exactly as you are. It lets you be who you are, care about what you care about, and not give a toss about things you're uninterested in and unbothered by. For example, 'Rob a massive bank tomorrow' might be the Double Best choice of a dedicated bank robber (no, the risk of imprisonment doesn't deter him). 'Fly around the world every week on my private jet' might be the Double Best choice of a multi-millionaire who doesn't care about saving the planet. And if you disapprove heartily of those two characters — if you're passionate about preventing climate change or creating social justice — then your

Double Best choices will inevitably reflect the high value you place on those causes.

However much you disapprove of bank robbers, I hope you can see the immense value of a decision-making tool that is structurally non-judgemental. When we try to prevent people from being who they are and wanting what they want, we force what they know to be true about themselves into the darkness. That makes it much harder for them to make good decisions without anxiety and second-guessing — and we do this to ourselves all the time too: 'I shouldn't want this', 'Isn't it terrible that I'd prefer X to Y?', etc. The absence of moral judgement in the formula signals that it's safe for us to take a profoundly honest look at what we like, dislike, yearn for and fear.

That's the manifesto part done. I don't know about you, but I'm convinced. And now it's time to see how The Double Best Method holds up in the face of some quite challenging choice-making provocations…

Chapter 11

Some Double Best Case Studies

Let's start with some easy ones:

The Movie

An independent film maker declared himself keen to make a movie version of *The Mystery of Mr. E*, the murder mystery musical that I had co-written with my friend, composer Annette Armitage. This director had all the enthusiasm, skill, energy and connections that would enable him to make the film, but he did not have a budget. My choice was between the following:

Option 1 — Give him the money he needed to fund the making of the movie.

(- - - Best Possible Outcome: he makes a movie based on Annette's and my musical that is both brilliant and a huge success. And by funding it myself, I get to 'be my own Steven Spielberg'.)

Option 2 — Don't give him the money to make the movie.

(- - - Best Possible Outcome: I have a brilliant and successful rest-of-my-life that does not include a movie being made of *The Mystery of Mr E.* Or perhaps Actual Steven Spielberg turns up one day, buys the rights to the musical and makes it into a movie.)

This choice was a no brainer for me. By a huge distance, my favourite of these two BPOs was number 1. No offence whatsoever to Steven Spielberg, but if I'm choosing between the chance of a success via his help and money, or the chance of a success that comes from me backing the project financially myself (and by extension, having considerably more control over it), I'm going to choose the latter every time. Why? Because it requires so much more of me in terms of: self-belief; giving myself permission; being the person who decides that my creative product is worth it without waiting to see if any of the 'big guns' agree with me; being the authority in my own life; being Panglossian in my conviction that if I fund this movie for all these reasons that I love, then everything is bound to work out brilliantly.

Also, the fact that I financed the movie entirely on my own, without a single pound or dollar from anyone else, would be viewed as outlandish and outrageous by many people. Writers simply do not do this — not even the ones who are multi-millionaires and could easily afford to. (Hopefully some of you remember from an earlier chapter that I love to be outlandish and outrageous if at all possible. And I would love to think that my bizarre decision to spend a huge amount of money on making my own movie might prompt other writers to do the same. Think about it, Other Writers: why have we all been sitting around hoping, waiting for Spielberg or Hitchcock or Scorcese to come to us, and assuming that, if they don't, we cannot have a movie made of our amazing book/play/musical?)

The WPO attached to Option 1 was: the movie is made and is terrible. I hate it and can't stand to mention it or show it to anyone, ever. Some people say to each other, 'That movie of Sophie Hannah's musical was awful, wasn't it?'. So what? Big deal! I was absolutely willing to take the risk of this happening in order to imaginatively inhabit the BPO of Option 1 for as long as possible. I'm not at all afraid of people saying that my creative products are awful. It happens all the time. Some people love my books and others hate them, and that is as it should be. I've already learned how not to give the slightest toss if other people, or if I myself, do not think that something I've created is good. I'm always focused on creating the next thing and making it as amazing as possible.

The House In Wales

My husband and I had to decide whether or not to continue looking on Rightmove for our perfect Welsh country house. My husband is half Welsh and our dog, Brewster (a Welsh Terrier) is entirely Welsh. We love Wales, and regularly rent houses there for short holidays. I was not at all convinced that we ought to buy a Welsh country house — not because I disliked the idea in theory, but because it felt like an additional complication that I didn't need in my life at that point. So, we put it through a Double Best analysis:

Option 1 — We keep looking on Rightmove for a Welsh country house.

(- - - Best Possible Outcome: we find one we adore, fall madly in love with it, decide that our passion for it makes any additional life complications more than worthwhile, and end up with a property in Wales that brings extra joy into our lives.)

Option 2 — We stop looking on Rightmove for a Welsh country house.

(- - - Best Possible Outcome: we save time that we might have spent *not* finding our perfect house, and we spend that time doing something else that leads to amazingness. We eliminate the possibility of all that extra complication and admin. Also, we give ourselves the opportunity to feel joyful while not owning a Welsh country house, and learn the important lesson, in case we had forgotten, that our thoughts, not our houses, create our feelings.)

This was an interesting one, because I was pretty sure I did not want to buy a house in Wales at that point. However, a Double Best reckoning soon revealed that Option 1 was the clear winner here. Why? Several reasons:

1) The WPO of Option 1 (missing out on our perfect house, that we would have fallen head over heels in love with if only we'd seen it) was not, in my

opinion, worth risking, given that the *action* involved in choosing Option 1 was nothing more and nothing less than…something I loved doing. My favourite hobby, in fact: browsing Rightmove.

2) Choosing Option 1 (and spending ten minutes every three days or so looking at Welsh houses online) was in no way going to stop me doing anything and everything else I might want to do.

3) (This was the most persuasive factor of all.) If we found our perfect house, fell for it hard and thought, 'We simply must have it! This is destiny!', then I knew I would, in that instant, switch from being someone who did not want to buy a house in Wales to being someone who did. And if that happened, I knew that New Me wouldn't mind the admin or the complications — because I'm willing to put up with almost anything in the service of Massive Love of a Destiny-ish Kind.

A Double Best analysis made it clear to me that the true choice here was not: 'Do I, right now, know that I want to buy a house in Wales?', but rather: 'Do I want to keep putting myself in the position where I might at any moment discover that I desperately want to buy a house in Wales?'

Once I realised that was the question, I saw that there was no significant WPO associated with answering 'Yes'. If I kept looking, I would either a) find a house in Wales that I loved, and buy it, b) find a house in Wales that I loved, and fail to buy it because someone else got there before me, or c) never find a house in Wales that I want to buy.

All of these made me think, 'So what? I'd still be fine.' Yes, I might be heartbroken if I found my perfect Welsh house only to have it snatched away by a quicker mover or higher bidder, but so what? I've been heartbroken a gazillion times before, and I've got over it. I'm not afraid of the pain of loss, and it's certainly not a good enough reason for closing myself off to the possibility of new, amazing house love.

The Forgiving Of The Bad Behaviour

I was involved in a project a while ago that mattered hugely to me. Without my cooperation, it could not have proceeded. However, the main person I needed to cooperate with had sub-optimal communication skills, neurotic tendencies and a mild persecution complex, which led to her treating me very rudely and unfairly on three occasions. She apologised for the second, but she neither apologised for the first and the third, and nor did she realise that she had done anything wrong at all on those two occasions. If the project's welfare and success had not been at stake, I would have ended my relationship with her at this point. My choice was:

Option 1 — Tell her I don't work with people who treat me in this way, especially not when it happens three times, and end the relationship.

(- - - Best Possible Outcome: I feel great about having enforced my boundaries and demonstrated that I will not stand for being treated poorly. I go from being someone who will put up with other people's crap sometimes to being someone who will not.)

Option 2 — Say nothing about her bad behaviour, smile and be nice, and do what I have to in order to make the professional relationship work, and by extension the project.

(- - - Best Possible Outcome: the project proceeds and is a huge success, and she ends up behaving better after my delightful and cooperative demeanour finally makes her chill out and be less neurotic. We end up having a great and ongoing professional relationship because I haven't walked away, and I really enjoy working with her as soon as she starts mirroring my good behaviour and being more reasonable and less rude.)

I chose Option 2 for one reason and one reason only: the WPO of Option 1 was 'Our project is over before it's begun', and I judged that to be an intolerable prospect — not quite at the level of getting eaten by crocodiles or squashed by a falling hippopotamus, but almost.

Since I decided to suck it up and make it work, she has only behaved badly to me on one occasion and it was an extremely minor offence compared with the previous three. We now have a great working relationship because I make allowances whenever I need to and remind myself of my Double Best choice and how right it was. Part of what makes our dynamic work is that I now fully expect her to do unacceptable things occasionally. I'm very happy with my choice to accept the unacceptable sometimes, in order to give this project its best chance of success.

All of these three examples were easily resolved in my mind when I applied The Double Best Method.

§§§

Now let's look at two 'live' examples. Both of these are still undecided — deliberately so, because I wanted to put them through the Double Best process in real time. Let's see what happens…

The Liking Or Disliking Of Amelia

(Many of the details of this one have been fictionalised, but the essential choice involved is exactly as presented.)

Amelia, my brother's wife (I do not have a brother; this is one of the fictional bits!), secretly sells his clothes, headphones, bikes and trainers, lies to him about it, and uses the money to buy illegal drugs. Whenever my brother finds out she has done it again, he's devastated — but he adores her and so he forgives her and stays with her.

I dislike Amelia intensely, mainly because of the pain she has caused my brother, but also because I think her behaviour is reprehensible. The mere thought of her causes a lava-like, burning rage feeling to rise up inside me and block my chest and throat so that I can't breathe. I really, really wish that my brother would divorce Amelia.

I am also aware that Amelia is probably doing the very best she can, doesn't mean any harm, is acting out her own trauma in some ways, and genuinely loves my brother. There is evidence that she might view him as her soulmate, and he certainly thinks she is his.

I could choose to stop loathing Amelia with a white-hot passion, and instead feel compassion for her and train myself to like her for her many sterling qualities. She is far more than a lying, thieving propper-up of the illegal drugs trade; she is also clever, funny, sensitive, kind and in many ways — in every way apart from the lying and stealing, in fact — a thoroughly good person.

I have, several times, advised my brother to divorce Amelia, mourn the loss of the relationship, and then go out and find someone to love who doesn't lie to him and steal from him constantly. He has, so far, not done this because he loves Amelia too much, so the current situation is that I dislike my brother's wife, to whom he might well be married forever.

Here is the choice I face:

Option 1 — I resolve to start liking Amelia immediately, and get to work thinking all the positive thoughts I can about her in order to reinforce my new, chosen opinion.

(- - - Best Possible Outcome: My brother and I are of one mind: we both love Amelia, and feel united in relation to her, not divided. I stop feeling guilty for not trying to change my current beliefs. I stop thinking I'm being mean or stubborn or superior for disliking her. I know my brother would be thrilled if I stopped negatively judging Amelia and started to love her, and I would be happy to think I'd made him as happy as possible, especially since Amelia is making him so unhappy. Also, I will feel cheerier and calmer about the fact that my brother is married to Amelia if I love her than if I don't — and I like feeling contented and peaceful.)

Option 2 — I decide it's fine for me to carry on disliking Amelia, and I do so.

(- - - Best Possible Outcome: my brother and I remain close even though we disagree about this one thing; I never say anything mean about her to him, and never again suggest that he should leave her; I even say lots of nice, compassionate things about her wherever possible, as long as I think they're true — like 'Of course Amelia loves you — she's doing this because she's terrified of giving up drugs and needs to fund her habit somehow. And no, of course her intention is not to hurt you.' I can say all of this in good conscience because I think it's all true. But I also get to honour my current opinion and feelings about Amelia, and make peace with never liking someone who causes my brother such pain.)

Okay, so…which of those BPOs do I prefer? I'm honestly not sure. Do I want to make myself happy, calm and non-guilty by believing this new thought: 'Amelia is lovely and likeable and exactly who my brother should be with if they love each other, which they clearly do?' Or would I prefer the possibility that, for the rest of my life, I will have a sister-in-law whom I dislike?

That second one sounds pretty bad. Right, so does that mean I want to choose Option 1? Maybe. After all, I am keen on liking people, agreeing with people and promoting jollity and harmony wherever possible. The BPO of Option 1 sounds like a good bet, in which case.

So — next step: what's the WPO of Option 1? I put aside my own principles and values about right and wrong ways to behave, and end up liking someone who has caused, and continues to cause, immense pain to my brother.

No thanks. That actually made me feel nauseous when I considered it. However upsetting it is to dislike my brother's wife and disagree with him about her, it would be considerably more painful for me (right now; maybe one day I'll be super-enlightened and want to love absolutely everybody) to try to brainwash myself into liking someone whose actions are creating such suffering for my poor brother, and who shows no sign of changing her tune any time soon.

Meanwhile, let's check out the WPO of Option 2: I continue to dislike Amelia, feel guilty about it, and think I'm an unforgiving harpy and that it's a problem if my brother and I disagree about her. But wait: I don't need to believe or do most of those things. I'm in charge of that.

How about: I continue to dislike Amelia (unless she truly changes her ways, of course), I stop feeling guilty for this perfectly valid opinion, honour my own intellectual and emotional truth, support and love my brother (including by not saying anything mean about Amelia, ever again), and choose to think that no pair of siblings, however close, agrees on absolutely everything?

Choice made! Notice how this decision doesn't require me to be more ready to forgive and love all humans unconditionally than I presently am. The Double Best Method works perfectly for my current, flawed self. And going through the process reminded me of an important point I've not yet covered: whenever you're choosing between BPOs and asking yourself if WPOs are worth risking, always notice your bodily reaction. If there's an outcome that makes you feel physically sick, take that seriously. And if there's one that brings tears of joy to your eyes, pay attention to that too. Our bodies often know before our minds do what we do and don't want to happen, and they find all kinds of interesting ways to share this information with us.

Let's move on to Live Decision Example 2…

The Zoom On Holiday Dilemma

I have a five-day holiday coming up in Italy. It's been booked for nearly a year, and I've made sure to put absolutely nothing in my diary for those dates, apart from 'Holiday'. It's very important to me that I will be doing no work at all during those five days — not even checking emails. I hardly ever give myself a complete break and have not done so for more than a year, so this really matters to me.

Last week, a course I'm doing changed one of its online class dates — from the day before I fly to Italy to the day after I land, the first full day of my holiday. So my choice is:

Option 1 — Ask the course instructors if it's okay if I miss that one session and catch up later.

(- - - Best Possible Outcome: they say, 'Yes, of course,' and I get to have my full, uninterrupted five-day holiday with their blessing. I catch up by watching the recording of the class later. I ignore my tiny fear that they will interpret my request as a lack of enthusiasm or commitment to the course, and, by ignoring it, prove to myself that we can be scared of things and still do them, if we like our reasons.)

Option 2 — Tell the course instructors that I'll be missing that one session because I'm on holiday, and will catch up later.

(- - - Best Possible Outcome: I get my full, uninterrupted five-day holiday with my own blessing, reinforce in myself the knowledge that I don't need anyone else's approval, and catch up by watching the recording of the class later. I don't worry at all about whether the course directors interpret my absence as a lack of enthusiasm or commitment to the course because I know that I'm 100% keen and committed, and that's all I need.)

Option 3 — Attend the session from my hotel room, or from beside the swimming pool, while on holiday.

(- - - Best Possible Outcome: I have a 100% attendance record, no one would even dream of questioning my enthusiasm or commitment to the course, and I enjoy the session as a part of my holiday, rather than viewing it as an interruption to it. I would not need to contribute anything apart from my attention, since normally I have a tendency to over-contribute, if anything, so I could watch the class as if it were a fascinating and entertaining movie and make it a fun part of my holiday.)

I already know what my Double Best choice is here, before even asking myself about any WPOs. It's Option 3. Why? Because as I was typing out Options 1 and 2, and writing the words 'Catch up by watching the recordings later', I realised that the video of the class would be sent out almost immediately after the class finished, and that I would *for sure choose to watch it while still in Italy.* Why? Because these classes are suspenseful, dynamic, unpredictable. They are, in many ways, like episodes of the most fascinating drama ever. (Of course. Would I choose a boring course to do? No, I would not.)

So given that I'd be super keen to watch the replay as soon as it was sent to me, and given that I know I would worry a bit about spoiling my 100% attendance record, whether I 'ought to' or not, the answer is obvious: I might as well attend the session in 'watcher' mode. That's my BPO — making attending the class in person a fun part of my holiday.

What's the WPO there? 'Missing' some of my holiday? But I won't be. The Zoom will be part of my holiday, an extra dimension to it. How about: letting myself down by allowing work to creep into my holiday? That sounds so plausible, doesn't it? But it doesn't convince me, because watching something I'd want to watch as soon as possible for fun anyway is not, to my mind, work.

I hope everyone noticed there that, *en route* to my Double Best choice, I got to think about what concepts like participation, work, holiday and fun meant to me.

In the next chapter, we're going to look at a few more ways to use The Double Best Method as a springboard for deeper analysis.

Chapter 12

Taking The Double Best Method Deeper

The Double Best Method can be incredibly simple, but it also allows us to delve much much deeper into the complexities of choice-making situations, should we wish to do so.

The following exercises will help you to gain clarity around questions like 'Is my Worst Possible Outcome worth risking?' and 'Which is truly my favourite of the available Best Possible Outcomes?'

Exercise 1) List the BPO and WPO for every option. In relation to each of these, ask yourself, 'And?' and 'But?'. List all the 'Ands' and all the 'Buts' you can think of for each one. How do they change your thinking about the decision?

Exercise 2) List the worst possible result of each BPO, and the best possible result of each WPO. For example, the worst possible result attached to the BPO of 'It doesn't rain and you're not carrying an umbrella around with y 'might be: 'I learn that I always get away with everything.' This might make you more likely to break into your neighbour's home and steal her favourite Persian rug!

Exercise 3) How many unquestioned assumptions and automatic beliefs can you find embedded in your decision-framing questions, your BPOs and your WPOs? For example: in the Umbrella scenario, the assumption is that rain is bad. Once you question this prejudice, you might find that you're happy to get soaked in between meetings in the city because you'd know that your partner, an arable farmer with a crop of wheat urgently in need of rainfall, would be jumping for joy.

Exercise 4) When thinking about BPOs and WPOs, make a distinction between outcomes you might create yourself, and outcomes that might occur but that would not be your doing or responsibility. For example, in my Zoom On Holiday dilemma from Chapter 11, my course instructors thinking I am not 100% committed to the course is a possible result that my decision/behaviour would not have created, no matter what I chose; only *they* can control what they think. Whereas me worrying about them thinking that, and creating anxiety for myself, would be a result *I* created. Notice if you find yourself favouring possible outcomes where you get to create more, or less, of the overall result.

As we saw in the *The Liking Or Disliking Of Amelia* example, part of what I wanted to resolve was whether I was more responsible for my dislike of her, or whether she was. I ended up concluding that, yes, my thoughts about her were 100% my responsibility *and...*I would have felt intolerably irresponsible if I'd tried to like her, given that her attitude and behaviour offend my values at a soul-deep level.

Do you lean towards wanting to be more responsible for outcomes, or less responsible? Why do you think that is, and do you want to change it? I sometimes consciously choose in favour of possible outcomes where I will inevitably be less responsible for whatever happens — for instance, if I feel I've been in charge of something for too long and believe it's time for someone else to take the reins.

Exercise 5) It's always extremely useful to ask ourselves, 'How do I want to feel after I've made this decision?' and then to look at all our options and ask ourselves which of them will be most likely to produce that emotion or combination of emotions. In the case of *The Liking Or Disliking Of Amelia*, I wanted to feel less anger and pain, and I realised that trying to like her would only make me feel more of both.

Chapter 13

Questions and Objections

I love questions. I love objections. Instead of hiding from them, or trying to banish or repel them, I want to seek them out, frame them to myself in the most reasonable and well-argued way that I can, and then see if I can answer them all adequately.

So, now is the moment for all quibbles and queries to step forward. Let me tackle you one by one!

1) The Double Best Method isn't necessary in all cases.

Agreed. If you're in the vegetable aisle at the supermarket, choosing whether you'd like broccoli or cabbage to go with your sausages tonight, then just decide which you'd rather eat and buy it. There's no need for a step-by-step process when the only upsides and downsides are 'I eat my preferred green vegetable' and 'I don't eat my preferred green vegetable.' Choose, move on and never think about it again. Please don't spend hours asking yourself 'and' or 'but' in relation to broccoli versus cabbage.

2) The Double Best Method doesn't work in all cases.

Yes, it does. If both BPOs are equally attractive, toss a coin. If none of the steps and no amount of taking it deeper helps you to decide, then tossing a coin will be just fine as a way of settling the matter.

Now, some of you might be thinking, 'What if all the WPOs are so unbearably awful that no choice is palatable?' There are many thriller novels out there at the moment with this sort of dilemma at their heart, with shoutlines like 'Maria must choose: either her two beloved children get squashed to death by falling hippos, or a thousand strangers in Kentucky die of tuberculosis.'

If you are ever faced with a choice that you cannot bear to make because the WPOs are all horrific, you can always add the option 'I refuse to decide', and then pick that. Sometimes 'I haven't chosen to do either of those two terrible things' is the Double Best choice in a tough situation.

And in a scenario where the WPOs of choosing *and* refusing to choose are equally unbearable (let's say you and everyone else involved will be instantly killed whether you choose any of the options or refuse to choose), then The Double Best Method gives you full permission to reclassify that horrific 'choice' situation as Not A Choice At All, or perhaps as Non-Optional Awfulness Whichever Way You Turn.

The Method works brilliantly when there is a meaningful choice to be made, but it unfortunately does not solve the problem of 'Sometimes people are evil and life is unbearable.'

3) Isn't The Double Best Method just what our brains automatically do when making decisions?

In other words, don't we all think 'What do I want?' and then 'But what might the downside be?'

This is an element of our 'normal' decision making process, for sure. But we also, and constantly, second guess ourselves and think, 'What if I'm wrong to want X? What if I don't deserve Y? And what do other people think I should do? And what might happen if I do X, or Y? And what if I regret this choice in the light of future events?' Those unhelpful thought loops muddied the waters of my decision making for most of my life, until I invented The Double Best Method. Now, they no longer hold me up or weigh me down at all. You will be similarly unencumbered by nonsense considerations if you follow the Method.

4) Doesn't the Double Best Method make us too selfish, or greedy, or unrealistic, or overly ambitious? Or, perish the thought, Panglossian?

No. We never need to judge wanting whatever we want as selfish or greedy; it is not helpful to do so. Unrealistic? Nope. We're only stating what *might* be possible if we choose Option A over Option B; we're not thinking it's definitely going to happen. And we believe — or at least The Double Best Method believes — that it's worth aiming as high as possible, not only because we might get our most desired result, but also because of how we grow and evolve and have fun along the way. The Double Best Method is underpinned by a worldview that believes:

a) Choosing optimistically creates the best possible 'Experiential Results', because feeling happy and excited about our favourite possibilities is fun, regardless of outcomes.

b) Feeling happy and excited fills you with the correct fuel to generate the actions that will produce good outcomes. So optimism as a practice increases your ability to succeed.

c) Once you install the thought habit of believing good things are happening and will happen, you are far better protected against fail results than you otherwise would be. Because our brains are so reluctant to give up the happiness habit, they simply looks at fails and think 'Weird. Does not compute.' And then they turn their attention to the next thing they can find to feel good about.

5) What if I don't agree that using The Double Best Method will eliminate the risk of making a wrong choice?

What if you follow the Method to the letter and still end up agonising about whether you've chosen well — preferred the right BPOs, feared the wrong WPOs?

Yes, of course, you can always agonise and say 'What if I was a big fool?' But, two things:

a) Don't. Commit to not doing that. This is a thing you can choose to do, and there's an enormous benefit to choosing it.

b) There's a big difference between deciding in the moment, when the difficult choice is upon you, and planning in advance how you're going to approach such situations. If you've read this book, been persuaded that The Double Best Method is the key to making great decisions and resolved to use it as your decision-making policy henceforth, then you've pre-approved it. Why would you then wish to make yourself wrong for following the policy that you've officially endorsed and decided to implement? Regret, and worrying that you've chosen badly, are both far more likely if you have no system for decisions and are simply flailing around each time you face a new choice-making situation. They're also more likely to afflict you if you're the kind of person who is determined to make yourself wrong, no matter what you do and no matter which brilliant tool you are using. Following a foolproof process and then agonising about it afterwards is like driving from Scotland to Cornwall and then tormenting yourself with the notion that perhaps you could have got there quicker if you had only had watermelons attached to the bottom of your car instead of wheels. (Also, if the suspected wrongness of your preferred option is really going to bother you more than, say, choosing a different option would, then it won't end up being your preferred option.)

6) What if there's missing information, hampering our ability to see the full picture in a decision-making situation?

In that scenario, the absence of certain information becomes a simple fact in our collection of circumstances. Then we get to choose what we want to think or believe in relation to whatever we don't know: X, Y or Z. 'How do I want to fill in the gaps — with positive or negative speculation? And why?' could be a Double Best choice in itself, or part of a thorough Double Best analysis.

7) What if other people pressure me to choose their favourite option?

Say to those people, 'Thank you for your input, but I use an infallible decision-making formula to make all my choices and do not require feedback from anyone else.'

8) What if other people hear that I'm using The Double Best Method and accuse both it and me of being ridiculous.

Explain to them why it isn't and why you aren't. If you can't be bothered to explain, direct them to this book.

9) What if I try to practise The Double Best Method and get it wrong?

Yes, this might happen — and it's worth looking out for potential flaws in your Double Best practice. Below is a list of common errors to look out for:

a) Listing as one option something that is in fact several options — for example 'Talk to Wendy about the cat.' That is highly unlikely to be one option, because 'Talk to Wendy' could mean any number of things. It could mean, 'Wendy, I hate our horrid cat and want to give him away', or it could mean, 'Hey,

Wendy, do you think the cat might be happier living with your mother, who has a huge garden for him to roam around in? I do!'

b) Trying to fool ourselves that we're nobler, kinder, wiser and all-round better than we are when answering the Double Best questions. I helped a friend to do a Double Best analysis recently and it soon became clear that what she was telling herself she wanted most was the outcome she thought she *ought* to want most, but in fact did not want at all. Do not allow 'shoulds' to block you from seeing the truth.

c) Using The Double Best Method while doubting it, and constantly telling yourself that the very idea of a decision-making formula is silly. You have to respect The Double Best Method in order to get Double Best results. If you're using a system while simultaneously undermining your own faith in it, you're not going to trust or even recognise the benefits you get.

d)   Not using The Double Best Method, or only using half-remembered bits of it. If you're going to do it, do it properly. Don't just think, 'What was that Double Best thing again? Something about favourites?', and then choose something you'll probably hate and blame it on the Method that you haven't followed properly.

e)   Rushing the Method in order to get to the answer quicker. If you rush it, and don't think deeply about each question and answer, then you'll skimp on the 'exploring your true thoughts and feelings part' and come up with the wrong answer.

If you make sure you're not doing any of these things, the Method will work — it's as simple as that.

The Wrap-Up

As you start practising this brilliant Method, it's important to celebrate your Double Best wins.

Wait. What does that mean?

Put down this book for five seconds and ask yourself: what constitutes a Double Best win?

How many of you thought that by 'wins', I meant 'times when The Double Best Method gave me an outcome I loved'?

I did not mean that, y'all. Come on, now. Obviously it's great when that happens. We all love that. And also…we don't need great outcomes-from-Double-Best-decisions in order to have huge wins with the Method. The decision itself — choosing your favourite possibility while feeling secure in the rightness of your choice — is the first and most important big win.

My latest significant Double Best win is that I've just invested in a company that, if all goes well, could succeed in a billions-of-dollars kind of way. How likely is that to happen? Well, based on what's happened already, it's statistically more likely to work out well than RoboDoc was, but the odds are still against us, I assume. But so what? According to the very clever scientist who first introduced me to this stellar species of algae (it's algae this time, folks, not surgical robots), the bio-fuel it produces when subjected to his special technological procedures might change the world and save millions of lives. Amazing!

My decision to invest was a massive Double Best Method win, no matter what the result for the company turns out to be. I'm already enjoying all the goodies: believing, hoping, imagining a future in which all planes and boats are powered by 'my' incredible algae's fuel…

And I'm well prepared for the exciting and uncertain journey ahead, because I packed my Double Best Kit Bag before I set off.

The top ten items you'll need to pack in your Double Best kit bag

1) A willingness to feel uncomfortable sometimes about the uncertain road ahead. ('I'm a bit nervous

about what might happen next. Of course I am —
that's perfectly normal. Who wants to loll around
complacently in the middle of their comfort zone?
Not me.')

2) A willingness to believe, in this new and nothing-to-
do-with-evidence way. ('Will I one day win
Wimbledon if I start having tennis lessons today?
Yes, I believe I will! No, of course I can't prove it,
silly. Yes, I know most Wimbledon winners start
playing tennis as children. You're not getting it. This
kind of believing relates to the future, so proof and
statistics have nothing to do with anything.')

3) A willingness to be the authority. ('I'm happy,
indeed eager, to take on board expert opinions
where relevant, *and*...no one knows more than I do
about what is the best choice for me.')

4) An understanding that if we get an outcome we
don't like, it in no way makes our decision
regrettable or a mistake. No Double Best decisions
'turn out to be wrong'; their rightness never
depended on outcomes. ('Obviously I'm sorry I
didn't manage to find a cure for rheumatoid

arthritis, but I'm pleased I gave it my best shot instead of glugging Tequila on a sun lounger all day.')

5) A commitment never to tell ourselves the lie that if we'd chosen differently, amazing things would have happened. ('Yes, I tried to run a marathon and broke my leg just before the finish line — but it's nonsense to think that if I'd trained for longer and waited till next year to enter, I'd have done better. Who knows what might have happened? I might have been crushed by a falling hippo halfway through the third mile.')

6) A commitment to learn and benefit in any way we can even from the outcomes we don't like. ('I ended up making a 50k loss when I sold my house, but here's what I learned: I would still have bought that house like a shot, even if I'd known I'd lose 50k when I sold it. I've learned that houses, for me, are about home, love, security and beauty, not profit.')

7) An understanding that 'keeping our options open' is an illusion. As is the idea that, when we choose, we're closing off possibilities. Each choice, followed

by action, takes us towards new possibilities. And not choosing, staying stuck in indecision, closes off plenty of exciting possibilities if you make it a lifelong practice, as so many people do. ('Yes, I'm closing off the possibility of happiness with Prince William by telling him I plan to elope with Lady Gaga. But just think what amazing options and choices my new post-elopement life will contain! Gaga, ooh la la!')

8) A determination to get the most fun, inspiration, adventure and juice out of every Double Best choice. ('I'm going to be making the absolute most of this adventure from the second it starts to the second it ends. What? Yes, I am drinking champagne and seeing if there are any small islands anywhere for sale. What do you mean, my book hasn't been accepted for publication yet. Who cares? I'm enjoying believing that it will sell for five million pounds in a massive auction, because — spoiler incoming, or maybe it's just foreshadowing — I understand there's no downside to optimism, ever.')

9) An understanding that there is no downside to optimism, ever. ('Who knew failing could be this

much fun? Right, now on to the next success-creation opportunity! Yay!')

10) A willingness to disregard what other people think about your choices, and to displease other people where necessary. ('Look, I know you'd prefer it if I would continue to be your cleaning lady — I understand you hate change and disruption and I sympathise — but I want to go to Nashville and become a country singer. I'm sorry you're upset, but I'm doing this because it's right for me.')

Right, then — is your kit bag all packed? Then go out there and Double Best your way to your most amazing life!

ABOUT SOPHIE HANNAH

Sophie Hannah is bestselling crime writer whose books are published in 51 countries and have sold millions of copies worldwide. She is the author of the new series of Hercule Poirot continuation novels, commissioned by Agatha Christie's family.

Sophie's murder mystery musical, 'The Mystery of Mr E', will be released as a movie on December 1, 2023. She is also a bestselling poet who has been shortlisted for the TS Eliot Award, a self-help writer, creator and host of the podcast How To Hold A Grudge, and founder of the Dream Author coaching programme for writers. She lives with her husband, children and dog in Cambridge, England, where she is an Honorary Fellow of Lucy Cavendish College.

And Sophie can be found online here:

Website: www.sophiehannah.com

Facebook: www.facebook.com/sophiehannahauthor/

Instagram: www.instagram.com/sophiehannahwriter/

Twitter: www.twitter.com/sophiehannahCB1

http://dreamauthorcoaching.com

https://podcasts.apple.com/gb/podcast/how-to-hold-a-grudge/id1439465411

Enjoyed this book? Read Sophie's How to Hold a Grudge

https://www.amazon.com/How-Hold-Grudge-Resentment-Contentment_The/dp/1982111429

Printed in Great Britain
by Amazon

22684761R00106